Special shout-outs and appreciation:

My family

Jorge Negrón

Orlando Plaza

Jesús Cepeda Brenes y Modesto Cepeda Brenes

José y Victor Emmanuelli

Julia Caridad y José Cepeda

Angél y Otoquí Reyes

Graphic artist Rafael Merino

Yasmar Cruz

Alex LaSalle

Manuela Arciniegas

All the cultural families in NYC and Puerto Rico

Instituto de Cultura Puertorriqueña

William Cepeda

Denise Solis

Cynthia Renta

Jorge Vazquez

LP21

To all the folkloric artists, educators, and cultural leaders in Puerto Rico, and the diaspora who work hard to preserve our culture. To those who are not mentioned here but know we have put in the work to share our Patria with others, you are loved, and greatly appreciated!

"In her debut work, "Homage to Moving Muses," Oxil Febles beautifully crafts a retrospective journal that seamlessly weaves together her journey, Afro Puerto Rican dance, culture, and the broader narrative of black identity. This book is a testament to the author's profound connection to her roots and the transformative power of the arts in shaping communities and individuals.

The strength of Febles' writing lies in her ability to vividly depict the intersectionality of her cultural experiences, growing up between the vibrant streets of East Harlem in New York City and the rich traditions of Puerto Rico. Through eloquent prose and insightful reflections, the author takes the reader on a compelling journey, offering a unique perspective on the Pan African Renaissance movement during a crucial time in the Caribbean and New York City history.

The use of Bomba as a central theme provides a rhythmic and thematic backbone to the narrative. Febles skillfully employs this Afro Puerto Rican dance and music form as a powerful metaphor, connecting disparate stories and highlighting how the arts have the potential to catalyze social change. The author's deep engagement with Bomba is not just a stylistic choice but a genuine reflection of her commitment to preserving and evolving Afro-diasporic traditions.

Oxil Febles' background as a teaching artist, folklorist, curator, and educator is evident in the meticulous attention to detail throughout the book. Her thirty years of experience shine through as she elegantly navigates the complexities of cultural diversity, tradition, and the transformative impact of the arts. The narrative is not only a personal retrospective but also a broader exploration of how the arts can catalyze societal evolution."

Table of Contents

Part 1

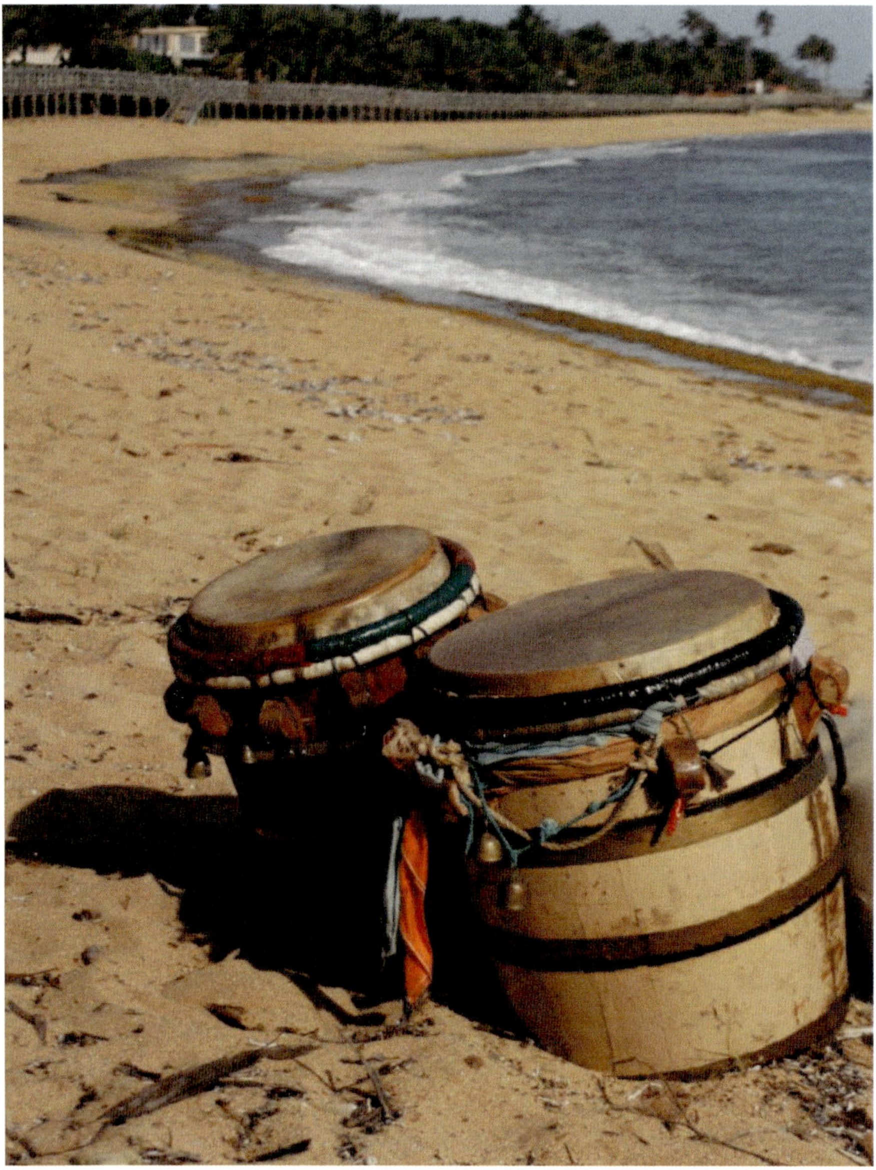

The Muse of Tales

The Muse of Tales

I hear folks say black and brown people should tell their stories. Well, here is mine.

En este mundo de tanto análisis y juicio sobre mis dioses negros y mi negritud laberíntica, existo y me muevo.Soy el secreto a voces de mi pasado que evidencia la violencia que creó mi mulatage y en ése limbo existo y me muevo. En este mundo donde nada es nuevo pero todo lo reinventado asombra, donde se predica paz violentamente, donde la gravedad insiste en que no me vaya pero el desapego es donde existe la felicidad, existo y me muevo. Aquí, en este plano donde la gente va y viene, donde las palabras se las lleva el viento si son buenas pero se plantan en la mente y el corazón si hieren, me muevo y existo. Aquí, donde todo tiene un código pero la moral no, me muevo y danzo. En este mundo donde mis ancestros crearon los caminos por donde mis muchos "Yo" nos paseamos, improviso la vida, la supervivencia, y en silencios y pausas creo otras rutas, shortcuts, setbacks, fuck ups, pero sigo moviéndome, existiendo, liberándome para alcanzar otras tablas existenciales en este juego called Life Time.

My story starts with the thought of me. It has to do with love, pain, deliverance, my ancestors, elders, traditions, movement, and stillness. It has to do with the two human beings that I chose as parents, and all the other energies that agreed to accompany me in this adventure. It is a story of oral traditions, about historical, hysterical chismes about what was, what is, and as we change, what will be.

Most of the things that I know about the first stages of my existence I owe to my family's stories about me. Some of the things that I know about them, and the people before them are also because of those moments of storytelling. I learned how important oral tradition was at an early age because I learned about myself through the memories, they shared about me growing up, which made me feel loved, and in return, those moments made me love them. My elders taught me about the existence of an invisible world that to them was more important than the physical one. They told me that whether

I liked it or not, accepted it or not, I was gifted with the blessing of the spirits.

I remember how my cousins and I sat around them to listen to la magia de los cuenta cuentos. They were great storytellers. Some of them were funny, others weren't, but all of their stories had a lesson about life's beauties and complexities. They taught me that we are all creators and characters of this beautiful story that bonds us. When we share these stories, we learn how time is not linear, we see the importance of other people in our lives, and how to move toward evolution.

Those stories were not ordinary anecdotes to me. My elders told them in a way that I lived them, and I can still remember their voices and gestures. They are also still meaningful and relevant. In this new adventure as I try to become a storyteller myself, especially for my grandson, I noticed how remembering can make us vulnerable, and how those memories take us to places and revive emotions that we can embrace and hold on to for a momento, or feel them and let them go for our sake. Although writing is new to me, and I am aware of the insecurity I feel in the process, I am okay sharing the interpretations of my memories in this raw form, en calma, y sin tiempo.

I guess it all started one evening when Mnemosyne visited me and I gave her a voice. She guided my hands to write her whispers as she took me on a retrospective journey. Once I began writing, suddenly other voices wanted attention and invaded my memorias. Memories that want to be known, sang, drummed, written, and danced for the purpose of continuity; for the purpose of reminding me to not forget my ancestors and elders. In that observance and understanding I find my essence and true calling. In that process, I had to take a closer look at my family, at strangers that became family, and family that became strangers. I went to places, relived events, and took a look at objects that shaped my worldview.

In this book, I pay homage to different muses who have inspired me. They have gifted me with the need to bámbula, and relive all the feelings attached to those recuerdos. As I revisited the past, I was very grateful with everything that life has given me. I felt humbled because

I have been graced with having good people that have blessed me with inspiring words, presence, support, dance, time, faith, love, power, and courage to believe in magical things. They have held my hand in this journey of dreams.

My life is a beautiful, moving mosaic where words in songs, poetry and conversations create images that float in my universe. A moving mosaic with images of many Puerto Ricos' in other nations, and a city in New York that replicates my island but with different seasons. Places filled with characters and plots that have stuck to my life and mutated into my personality and defined my values. Those muses are mirrors and in them I see myself, my culture, my people, the Patrias I grew up in, my womanhood, and my artistry. My muses refuse to stay on the sideline, silenced, watching my story being distorted and taken from me. They have forbidden me to stay still and let my contributions become invisibilized either and that is the reason of this work. In my moving mosaic, one of the muses that always reappears is Bomba. This beautiful art wanted me to take a moment to describe her differently, to see how she revealed herself to me, as a friend that has cared for me, and talk about her with love. She did not want to be dissected to be analyzed as something extraneous. I guess Bomba wanted to be remind me of how she has always been around for me and others.

With this journal I want to add to the existent narratives of the art I chose by inscribing my blackness in the way I feel it and was guided to do. This new place where muses have brought me, tied my thoughts in translations and divided my heart between two nations. Both of them my home, both of them black, complicated, interesting, and magnificent in their own right. On this trip with Mnemosyne, I had to revisit places where loved ones no longer exist physically, but are there waiting for me. Places where I had fun witnessing all the new things that were created for me, and where agridulce memories taught me about balance, to love what I had, who I was, and know when to go and let go. Those recuerdos have created una historia en mi cuerpo. A body filled with information, emotions, and meanings that waltz with others and life itself.

For all of that I thank the universe, Puerto Rico, New York City, and Africa. I thank the spirit of those who were brought to these lands against their will. I ask Olodumare and Yemaya to bless and forgive every soul that decided to free their spirit and save their temples from being desecrated in the name of greed on a cross. I honor what they left us, especially the knowledge of the existence of a spiritual world with so much to learn from. I thank my family, mi familia de sangre que me han dado tanto. I also thank all of those who have kept Bomba pulsing and have gone against all odds to pass it on to other generations. I want to thank and pay my respects to all of those scholars who dedicated their lives to rebuilding our past and informing us of facts that help us make sense of our present. I thank all the Puerto Rican women who have inspired me and the men who have taught me and supported me. I thank the different Bomba families in Puerto Rico who shared their knowledge, time, and moments of their lives with me and have become my extended family. My sincere appreciation and respect to all the talented musicians on the island and the Diaspora who have represented their love for Puerto Rico through their art by playing all of the music that represents us and with whom I have continued working for the culture. A special thanks to Mr. Orlando Plaza for all the work and years put into Camaradas, El Barrio, and for giving puertorriqueños a home away from home. My special thanks to Jorge Negrón for cultivating a space where Afro-Puerto Rican artists had a platform to express themselves and celebrate nuestra africanía. A place where Nandí broke a tradition, and created a new path in Bomba music in El Museo de la Raíz Africana. Thank you for the years of support and companionship in this journey of art and history. I thank everyone who has been a part of that cultural ride, and with whom I still have the blessing of sharing.

I dedicate these memories to the spirits that walk with me to honor and thank them for the force they bless me with. I also dedicate this work to my tribe who raised me and built the foundation on which I stand. To my Sun, Aris who is the greatest muse in my life. Having him as a son is the greatest gift God has given me. I gift this book to my grandson Akim in case we do not get to talk about these things, he can read these stories written by me and not someone else's interpretation of my life experiences. Gracias, Susana, my first dance teacher, grandmother and soulmate. I thank and send my eternal love to my mother's Olga and Migdalia; I am an extension of them. To my aunt Iris, who asked me to write, and all the women whom I have met throughout my life who have taught me what a true warrior is. All of those powerful people educated me and gave me the gift of freedom; a spiritual freedom that cannot be tampered with and nothing and no one can take away from me. Their legacy has pushed me to pursue my dreams, including this one. I dedicate this effort to my father and light, my guardian angels, the forces that are designated to protect me, and most of all to my God. That divine energy that has the shape of all things, including musical notes that deliver so many mysterious messages to those who listen. I thank that force for desiring to create me and for guiding me through a special purpose that she/he designed for me, and for sending those muses to my life to teach me something new. I thank that force for Bomba; cuya esencia e historia es Patria hecha danza y sonido.

Bless and be blessed.
Oxil Febles

Part 2

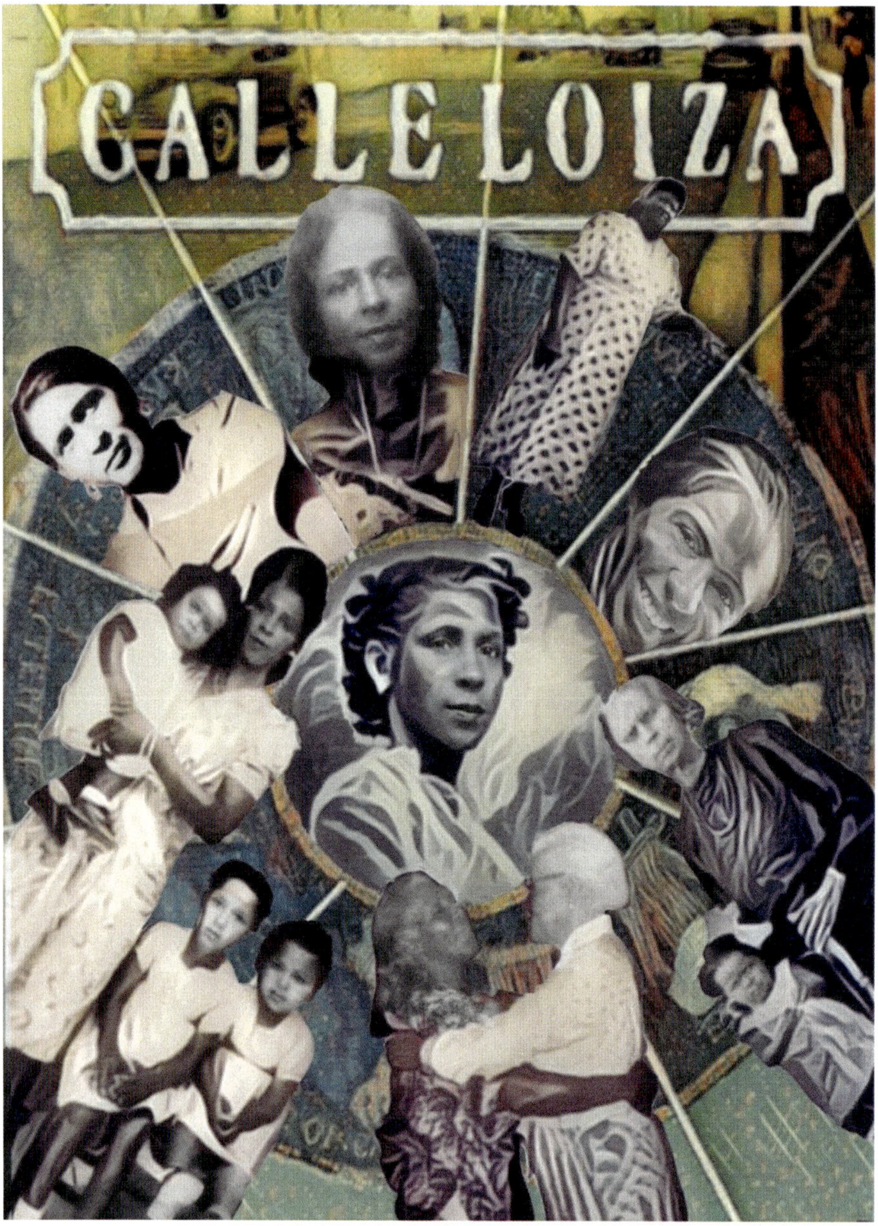
CALLE LOIZA

La Musa de la Calle Loiza

Dime de dónde eres y te diré quién eres

Ella no llega, ella aparece. Incense smoke danced in my living room to the sounds of the beat of a drum that comforted and grounded me. I gazed at the smoke forming spiraling shapes as it seduced me with its twirls. I danced like I usually do when I'm by myself. I dance differently because there are no rules, expectations, or restrictions. I followed the smoke, creating a choreography between us while we moved across the room. My smokey partner led me straight to my family pictures. As I stood there, I focused on a particular photograph that stood out. There she was, Susana Llano, my grandmother, staring at me with a beautiful smile. She always smiled when she saw people she loved and when she sang and danced. The frame focuses on her face at an angle where I can see her dimple. It is a black-and-white image that encases a collection of memories dear to me. It evokes a time when everything seemed as if life was just like that, black or white, good or bad, happy or sad, with no in-betweens because, for a kid, emotions are usually very defined and gray is hard to articulate. For my grandmother, times were rough in Puerto Rico, but she had many talents and grace. Like a professional dancer, she made those hardships seem easy to handle.

Susana was an admirable woman to me. I call her La Diva de La Calle Loiza. Canta Gallo is what they used to call the street where she grew up in Santurce. She walked around Calle Loiza as if she owned it. My family is very proud of being from that town. It has a great history of culture, commerce, art, and of the black families that built the foundation of San Mateo de Cangrejos (Santurce). People from Santurce usually ask others when they meet them for the first time, where are they from to know who they are, because the place where you come from is very important. The communities people came from had loads of information about families, legacies, and values. Growing up, Susana lived in various places but all of them in the streets near Calle Loiza.

Susana is a timeless woman who reappears unexpectedly in my life to lift my spirit, warn me about something, comfort me, protect me, and inspire me. She is not physically with me but she has never left me. We meet in dreams, whispers, premonitions, silence, a soft breeze, a sweet scent, a chill, and sometimes in visions so real that startle me. After my incense dance, I reminisced about our irregular connections. Distance has never limited our relationship, if anything, moments of separations connected us more. She taught me how a spiritually gifted person does not mind distances to communicate with loved ones. She taught me how to prophesize using a deck of cards, water, or just sitting silently connected to a higher power. She told me how spirits, like shapeshifters, can present themselves for good or bad, and we need to be in tune to have discernment. These things might seem deep, but when a person is exposed to this information at an early age it is easier to understand. Looking at her picture, still and silent, I felt her around me, and her presence reassured me that it was time for a new kind of movement and ways to remember her, them, us, and in due time, for others to remember me.

I learned from her and other women in my family the importance of dance. I adored it when she danced around me, with me, and lately, within me. I took in her image from the picture, and with it I felt love and gratitude for all the joyful moments she filled my heart with and the great inheritance she left me.

Susana was the youngest of all her siblings. She was the daughter of Obdulia Millán and Agustín Llano. She was born looking like a little Tongolele. I later learned that kids born with gray hair are called "Moses' children". She was born with a spot of gray hair on her hairline, which spread out like Ivy and blended with her dark hair, taking over more and more space faster than she probably would have wanted. I never thought about her within the concepts of time or age. She had great genes and a beautiful body. What I loved the most was her rich chocolate-brown skin. Susana was very feminine and took great care of every detail about herself. She taught me that the body is the temple of God, so I guess seeing her take so much care of herself was not about vanity; it was an act of gratitude to the divine. By watching her, my mother, and aunts, I learned to do the same. I loved her smile, her spirit, and her energy. She could not be overlooked. I remember Susana loved her siblings very much and respected them. My grandmother liked dancing with her sisters and singing with her brothers. They all knew how to make time stop and create worlds that kids and adults imagined vividly. One of the anecdotes that she shared with me, and that I enjoyed a lot, was when she used to follow her brothers when they went on their escapades. Her brothers used to go to certain places in Cangrejos where they watched people dance and play something called Bomba. My grandmother was the first person to mention that word to me, and like a password, Bomba has given me access to many spaces where my grandmother seems to be waiting for me.

Susana recalled those memories and tried showing me what Bomba was. I was a child back then, but those stories always stuck with me. I learned from her that Bomba was a dance, a special kind of dance and music. She repeated the same story on different occasions in my life as a reminder of something that one day I would need, and would have to look for or it would look for me.

I guess Bomba was something she got to like, and being who she was, maybe she knew before I did that Bomba would become one of those things that would connect us later on in life. As she recreated with words the images, sounds of instruments, and the steps she saw in those adventurous outings, I tried to imagine the scenes of a niña traviesa following her brothers. After some years, I was able to see what she spoke about, and I must say that my imagination fell short. I did not come close to what she meant and what Bomba looked like, sounded like, and most of all how it felt. Bomba has to be experienced, there is no other way. My grandmother grew up during a time when Bomba was done by black people in black towns in Puerto Rico. Everyone in those days knew what it was, how to dance it, or had an idea, and knew where to go to see it. It was no big a deal back then, unlike now that some people need to mention that they are related to so and so to claim a status. Back then that was not necessary. It was a normal thing among black folks to do Bomba until it wasn't. As a matter of fact, because it was a cultural expression among black Puerto Ricans, not many people seemed to care for it; not even black people. Bomba became less visible. This change maybe had to do with conditioning and the stigma that might have been attached to it that made people not want to identify with it, or the political agendas that later became laws imposed on Puerto Rico by the US. Perhaps it had to do with the way that predominantly black communities in Santurce were destroyed by expropriation and appropriation, that changed Santurce's infrastructure, and therefore made Bomba subside. For all those reasons and others that have to do younger generations and cultural changes, Bomba seemed to be less practiced and many people were forgetting it. At least my grandmother got to see it and shared it that memory with me. I remember my mother and my grandmother saying that Susana's older sister, Providencia, did not like Bomba. She preferred *Minuet* and other types of music that she enjoyed more. When I talk with my family about our elders, we say jokingly that they were uppity negroes. Eran negros orgullosos, which seems to be a common attitude amongst black people from Santurce. They are black Puerto Ricans who are proud, hard-working, very knowledgeable of the arts, and well educated. They have a grace, a certain style, a je ne sais quoi that identifies them. The environment had an impact on Santurce's children, and that defined people's style, and also the style of la Bomba from Santurce. My grandmother and her siblings might have had different musical preferences but all of them loved music. I loved watching them share those moments when they sang and danced. I often miss those times when I witnessed their joy, and how they shared their love through rhythms, songs, and dance, which made it all about the moment and the importance of presence.

When my grandmother danced, no matter the genre, she moved the same. Her dance consisted of agile, graceful footwork patterns that allowed her to mark every beat of the "clave" and percussion beats. I never saw her use a skirt as a prop to dance anything. As a matter of fact, Susana liked wearing pants. I believe she was living a transitional period when women wore dresses as a social norm, but pants slowly made their way into women's closets. She wore pants often because she believed to be a modern woman, but when she wore dresses, she looked as if she floated. Pants, back then, represented a woman's social evolution and an act of resistance, and Susana rocked her pants with style. With a dress or with pants, my grandmother looked beautiful. She also had good character and depending on her mood, her temper was not to be messed with. She grew up when people were not afraid to use a machete, and she handled hers very well, and ladylike while doing so. Her moves, whether dancing or walking around the backyard with her machete while telling stories, giving orders, or telling jokes were alluring. I think she must have been a daughter of Oshun.

When she danced, she combined gestures and poses, creating patterns and figures that were contained in a space that expanded slowly and elegantly. When she danced, it felt as if I was watching a movie. She would ask me to dance with her, and I would join her, feeling bashful because I knew I was entering a powerful and honorable space. One of the things she taught me, and that later made more sense as I participated and witnessed different dance circles is that people do not know what might be happening spiritually or energetically in those spaces to interrupt the process. It would be safer and appropriate to allow the dancer to do what they need to do, let them give closure to their dance, and allow the energy to flow before jumping in or interrupting.

Susana used to say that no matter how inclusive a space was, it was important to take some time to observe closely before getting in them. In time I understood what she meant. Sacred spaces are not always inside temples, and spiritual work and multiple traditions are performed in many ways and in places we might not even imagine. She taught me to create my sacred spaces and to take care of myself while sharing with others. She and I, in the middle of laughs, swirls, music, "espiritísmo", and lots of love, created many things and our little utopias where love was the only rule. We talked about dreams, futures, the past, and the present as if time did not define them. I cherished our closeness and her teachings, but I must say that what I enjoyed the most was to watching her dance. That was one of our rituals. I began taking in different things about her that, as a child, whether I was aware of it or not, they built in part my identity as a woman and a dancer. When I dance, I find her and I also know she dances through me. She had a deeper understanding of life and music. She used to say that not everyone knows how to listen and music requires people to learn how to listen first to be able to appreciate, and the body to respond. Most importantly my grandmohter, my mother, and most people in my family taught me to listen to silence. It might sound weird, but silence is good, and when children learn to appreciate that, they discover a new world.

As a *Medium,* Susana knew how to listen very well. Hearing and listening are not the same. She experienced being in different worlds simultaneously because she would be in one place physically, and mentally she would be in another space or dimension, which required a tremendous amount of concentration and openness to be able to listen to the messages of the universe and deliver them with clarity while being present in another. I think she applied those skills to the way she appreciated music. She also spoke a lot about melody. En la melodía está el sentimiento, she would say, and ask me to listen carefully because in silence you also find feelings.

Her appreciation for music and singing with her brothers taught me how important melody is to be able to create an emotion. In my opinion, melody impacts the music, the expression of dance, and also others that witness these expressions. How black folks talk carry certain melody that even when they speak, they sound as if they are singing. When storytelling, how people speak is as important as the content. Melody produces a feeling and that helps us connect to words, and it also impacts how we move.

Those experiences of listening to music with my elders helped me develop what musicians call oido musical. This concept is important for any dancer because, mostly in percussion-based music like Bomba, if the melody is not there, you need to search for something besides the rhythm to express in your dance. You need to connect to something in the music, which is usually the basic rhythm, but sometimes that is not enough, so the chorus and how the person sings play an important role. The melody that the singer creates, together with a musical base, creates the mood for the dancer to work on their improvisation and add to that musical composition while collaborating in the creation of a collective feeling. Although my grandmother was not a professional singer, people of her time knew how to harmonize and loved to sing in trios, which required an innate talent or lots of practice. As far as I remember, my grandmother and her brothers knew how to harmonize when they sang. They did it beautifully and had a keen understanding of finding each other in the tones and notes. Another detail was that she loved to play the guitar. Susana had a guitar that was her evening companion. Her guitar waited for her faithfully every night and surrendered to my grandmother's arms and curiosity. She was not a pro, but she liked experimenting with it and knew the basics. Susana played simple things with different sounds that informed her body, and that was revealed in her dance and her singing.

As a kid, I could not articulate what I felt or thought about when I saw her play and tune the guitar, but in retrospect, I find it poetic. I always thought my grandmother had a gypsy side to her and that I inherited too. While she played her instrument, I fell in love with it. I remember her holding the guitar, both of them bringing to life stories of nostalgia, romance, and peace, as if the oppressor's guilt, trapped in a guitar, asked the oppressed for forgiveness in the form of sounds. Honestly, I never saw her play a full song because I'd always fall asleep before she finished. She chose the moon and her muses to be a witness of that magical bond.

I remember her evening musical rituals. Her bed was high, or maybe because I was a child, I thought it was. Her room was always clean and smelled like a sweet scent. She held her curvy instrument that looked like her body, and I would lay next to her. A tall palm tree danced to her music and shared with us a cool evening breeze that seemed to know when and what to do when it heard the guitar. Those moments were even better when the smell of rain and wet grass invaded the room. She played, and as she did, her image faded slowly as I dozed off with the sounds of a Spaniard guitar whispering sweet nothings in my ear and the humming of songs of her youth. Her image would disappear before my eyes like a black Madonna that watched over me and my dreams. Those moments that would take her back to her youth created peaceful moments for herself while gifting me with memories that I can relive many times over.

I used to watch her walk from one room to the next, singing or talking to herself saying that elves used to hide her stuff every time she forgot where she placed things. She walked as if a musical accompaniment was playing in her head and followed her around wherever she went. She was in tune with the universe's rhythm, and when she danced her moves spoke to my soul. Her dance was spiritual, ancestral, and personal. She always danced to the core of the music and lived to the core of what was in her heart. Her "Susana dance" revealed another side of her; her passion for life and determination to enjoy her freedom. She danced and celebrated the moment and moved to unknown dimensions. She made me wonder about the places where she might have been taken on those dancing journeys, and I later understood that the éxtasis came from a place of release and encounter.

I knew the movements she made belonged to her, and although I admired them, I knew they were not mine to appropriate. They were copy-written by her authority, her life's stories, and her body in the process of her life's experiences. When Susana danced, she was there physically, but her mind and spirit danced somewhere else. Her movements were natural and flavorful, and her dark brown body was enough to enhance them. Like a live painting, her body contrasted with all the other colors in the spaces where she danced, and every movement seemed right. Her body, while dancing or doing ordinary chores, told her story. She did not force it, she did not fake it, and she never constrained herself either. Nobody could dance holding her for a long time because she had to be gazed at. She had to dance by herself. She was a natural performer. Susana made me think that some people are meant to dance alone because they have to be observed and felt from a distance to capture the magic of the energy, they possess. To be able to do that is a powerful thing, and that was the effect she had on people. I remember there was something she did that I always found unusual. She made sounds with her mouth, trying to emulate percussive sounds while she danced and marked steps. "Prá, tucutú" were some of the sounds she made, and back then, I didn't understand why or where it came from until some years later those sounds found me on one of my trips back to Puerto Rico when I was around seven or eight years old.

Susana, time, and I shared many stories, dances, and blessings together. What she taught me, about life and movement, like other elders that I learned from, were lessons that needed to be interpreted from a different place, not just from the mind. When it comes to Bomba I have never read any information about it that taught me what my grandmother and other elders did because those teachings came without a word said. A look, silence, watery eyes, and sometimes cracked voices taught me more about them and the love they had for what they did than any explanation. There were moments when the connection with my elders was so strong that everyone else disappeared, and it was just us. In those moments of respect and trust, they revealed things they would not share with everybody, and that is precious to me.

Like sweet incense smoke when it fades and leaves its scent impregnated everywhere, when she stopped dancing, she left a feeling in my heart that has never disappeared. My beloved grandmother stopped dancing at some point because she couldn't. She had cancer and was in pain, but even while enduring all of that, she did it as best as she could. Susana passed away leaving a huge emptiness in my life. In that painful process of seeing my Madonna slowly evolve, I took in all of those special things she taught me and promised not to forget. I honor her wherever I am, while I stand, and until I pass. I am because of her and those before her. I am because of those who came after her and who have continued her teachings and legacy. Those who are the pillars that hold me and that I know that if I trace back to the beginning, I will find God.

I saw her mature in a space where she created time, energy, and memories for me until hers physically ended. I always felt awe watching her do what she loved, even if it was watching her favorite novelas, and I still feel the same as I see her photograph. She moved, and moved the people she knew. She loved music and enjoyed it until the only thing she could do was move her head to the beat of Salsa songs as she closed her eyes, leaving us to go to other places that she only knew. God gave me the privilege of having such a wonderful woman and a strong spiritual warrior as a grandmother, and her daughters to take care of me.

That evening, after I knew she had left my apartment, I sat down to process the feelings and message she left me with. That evening she said two words: Purpose and identity. Those two words inspired me to continue reflecting and writing about some of the many experiences that I value and hold dear to my heart. She reminded me that I am the product of a lineage of warriors whose transformations, sacrifices, joys, tears, and hopes made the caminos where now I walk on, and I need to smooth them down for mines. They left me a divine heritage that regardless of how it chooses to manifest, it has always showed up at the right time. I feel blessed that my elders shared their stories, songs, dances, spells, knowledge, time, and love with me. I feel grateful that they saw the potential in me to carry on a legacy of continuity and making sure they are remembered. Susana, our relationship, her gift of Bomba, and what she represented in my life is still very much alive.

My experience with Bomba started with her story, her body, and her dance. My grandmother was the one who inspired me to see Bomba as a woman. Her beautiful, black, dancing body was a personification of Bomba to me. It was not about a dress or a skirt, it was about an essence. I see Bomba as a dancing woman who moves gracefully with everybody, in everybody, no matter the gender, age, or skin color, and also dances everywhere. It is a dancing muse that manifests as it pleases, and only a few have learned to understand her. The same way dancers become mediums for Bomba, Susana was a medium for energies, a vessel for life, a temple for many divine things, and also a resisting soma with flaws to endure the hardships and pains that as a perfect, imperfect being she needed to deal with to survive, like Bomba has done for centuries. The connection between the two has lasted to this day which makes it hard for me to think about one without thinking of the other. Susana still moves and shows up. She comes and goes, free as the wind, free as musical notes of instruments played outdoors, and like beautiful choreographies, our lives synchronize in different spaces and moments, and the same happens to me with Bomba.

While I continue learning about the uniqueness of my body in movement and continue adding to a body of work, I learn about my purpose. While I appreciate the opportunities that I have been given, and the blessings of my elders, I bless others by teaching them about this magical, wonderful art. While I unlock the secrets of this music and reconnect with my ancestors, I discover in my body the sacred information that shows me who I am and where I need to be. As I keep dancing, creating, receiving, and sharing energy, I honor the roots that ground me in every Bomba dance, and I dance to a melody that I only can hear. I dance to the melody of a guitar drowned under the beat of drums. I dance to drums that claim my freedom, my right to be happy, whole, and eternal.

Bendición Susana Llano, mi guela.
Ibae.
Luz y Progreso

Part 3

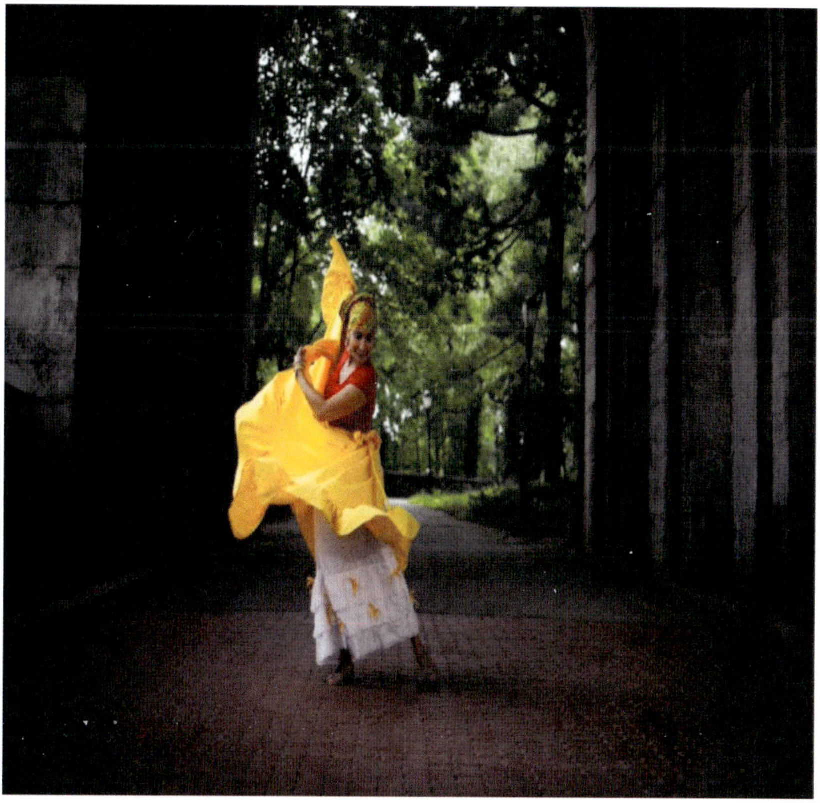

Soy Bomba

Soy Bomba

Bomba carries the weight of the souls of many that are still vibrating under deep waters and under the earth. Souls that come to life through the sounds of drums, played by mediums to liberate them. Bomba holds the ethos of a so-called primitive life by keeping a secret the prayers of our ancestor's survival. Prayers in codes that only Eshu, Olokun, and Olodumare understand.

Bomba is like a woman with a complicated history of mulatage that represents me. Bomba is a thread that stitches stories of survival, love, faith, and helped the enslaved Africans find a moment of life in the middle of a hell on earth in the name of a Lord. Bomba took them back home in a cipher they created with sounds, movements, and memories. Like a wise, ageless woman, Bomba refuses to be stuck in the past and becomes relevant in each stage of my life. She has stepped aside at times so I can have other experiences but always comes back for me if I don't look for her. She makes me look at her and makes me notice others, but mostly she makes me look at myself and I become others mirror.

Teaching this art has given me the blessing of reciprocity, and this book is a way of giving Bomba what she wants from me in this particular time in my life. Bomba is one of my ancestors, a friend, and my dance-or-die. I dance it, teach it, and have become her in many ways. I want to share the definitions that I have learned about Bomba, and the understanding that I have gained in my interactions with elders and Bomba. My understanding of Bomba changes with time, which has taught me how interesting and diverse this lady can be.

So, what is Bomba? I think Bomba is drums and voices that sound old, familiar, new for some, intense, bitter-sweet, deep, sometimes sad and black. Bomba sounds like an elder's voice calling you to dare to enter into different dimension where spirits sing and watch. Bomba is a cultural code that save lives and a universal code that connects us with angels and unknown gods. It is a musical foundation that, for some, is more than 400 years old, but in reality, Bomba is ageless.

Bomba is a secret, a desire; it is hope and prayers. Bomba is a story contained in a skin that rests on a barrel. Bomba is the hand that knows how to make the drum tell a story. Bomba is the hand that makes the call to wake up, rise up, show up, and be your authentic self, unapologetically, purposefully, and intentionally. It is the hand that makes the goat skin speak. Bomba is a sound that vibrates in a circle and has different effects on people and the environment where they find themselves. Bomba is survival.

Bomba is a feeling and an authority that will set the tone and control what happens in creative spaces without explanations. Bomba is a connector. It will connect you to something, a memory, history, space, the past, others, and yourself. It has the power to connect people to the cries and prayers of those who danced, drummed, lived, and died before us in what we call Puerto Rico. Bomba grounds those who migrate from the island and miss it. Bomba helps Puerto Rican immigrants to recreate their island wherever they are to feel whole, like the enslaved Africans did in the Caribbean centuries ago. We recreate a Patria through drumming, dancing, and songs. Bomba proves that Puerto Rico is not just land. It becomes other things that fill a void and create a sense of self, of belonging, and a root. Bomba is our root. Bomba is identity and the emotions attached to that. Bomba is the weight of that identity in our souls. Bomba is collective ancestry and the idiosyncrasies that make us who we are no matter where we are.

Bomba is Patria, in the places where we choose or need to be, even when being in Puerto Rico, because our colonized condition might create barriers that keep us away from having access to our land. Bomba is stories of our present struggles for a better future. Bomba creates dancing cyphers and cycles, and in them, history seems to repeat itself, and we do not notice. Bomba is a means of transporting people on journeys where they start and end in the same spot but with a different understanding of themselves. Bomba is fundamento, the basics of art and life. In that foundation, we meet elders and those who teach us about a common root back to Africa and to ourselves. Bomba is the dance of souls. It tells stories of sadness, joys, mischiefs, and mysteries transformed into danza. Bomba is like a Don Quijote book; depending on one's stage in life and interaction with it, the meaning gets more intricate, and one has more understanding of it. Bomba is a collective experience and also an experience of personal development. Bomba is a powerful teacher that can make people curious, anxious, and feel an uncontrollable need to learn more about it. Bomba creates a sense of ownership and control over it, as Bomba and the circles where she lives control you. Bomba is survival.

Bomba is a story about migrants. A forced migration stitches the common history between Africa, the Americas, and the Caribbean. Migration and the need for survival created Bomba, and all the expressions that we now refer to as La Diáspora. In the foundation of these expressions, we will find language, art, spiritual practices, and a tribal organization that connects us organically as a people. It connects us to Africa as a place of creation, which is more than just a continent. Bomba is Africa, Africa in Puerto Rico. Bomba is tradition and a source to make tradition evolve as it remains. Bomba is a technology that has evolved but always depends on the foundation for its continuance. Bomba is a presence and the exchange of energy in the presence of people. Bomba is attention, awareness, movement, but also stillness. In stillness, we can feel ancestral energy approaching us to give us strength. Bomba is survival.

Bomba is música de negros de Puerto Rico, national music that represents a group of people in the world. Bomba is part of Puerto Rico's history, a history that due to its blackness was ignored but like everything made by black people it became profitable. Bomba is still delivering people from bondage. Bomba is a product that can be capitalized and is constantly negotiated because, for the system and power that be, black people are still a commodity. Bomba is a mirror. Bomba is identity, race, and the politics of representation on and off stage. Bomba is the black body that represents it in all its shades and the stories of the lives of black people. Bomba is a platform for a nation's history and black people's visibility.

Bomba is collective remembrance and how people build new narratives of the same negritude. Bomba is a folkloric costume that impresses and also confuses. Bomba reflects the contradictions caused by biases that created a white-washed history. Bomba is oppression beautified on stage. Bomba is also the visibility and representation of black women in society. Bomba is an interdisciplinary and intergenerational art. Bomba is a mental space. Bomba is the richness of the people who built Puerto Rico, the wealth and identity of a rich port that was called Borikén and ceased to exist with its Taino's. Bomba is evidence of Afro-indigenous honor and African's loyalty to their motherland.

Bomba is dark-skinned and Creole, too. Es un mulatage forzado que crea divisiones por su historia y aún lo hace. Bomba is medicine for a trauma that we still deal with. Bomba was made to be human, feel human, heal the soul, and detach from the body and the circumstances. Bomba is movement and sound that decolonizes the body and the mind. Bomba is freedom. Bomba is community. Bomba is inclusive, but in principle, Bomba is black and belongs to black people. Bomba is complicated. Bomba is resistance and a way of life. Bomba is money. Bomba is dignity. Bomba is unconscious spirituality. Bomba is judgmental and territorial. Bomba is preservation and evolution. We preserve it and work for its continuity to keep a tradition that is in the process of a constant transaction with the status quo with the purpose of constructing an identity that also requires to be fluid because of Puerto Rico's political status.

Bomba is a trend, a mission, and a collection of experiences danced and drummed under palm trees, in front of beaches, parks, plazas, next to skyscrapers, and old buildings where everyone becomes one or not, but still, everyone sees her, La Bomba. Bomba is a woman who has given birth to many Puerto Ricans in different places and has multiplied. Bomba is a muse that inspires people with different things and redefines their history. Bomba is educational, a catalyst to change the narrative of black Puerto Ricans and their communities. Bomba is multidimensional and has crossed a timeline that creates these connections between the times. Bomba is cimarrona. She escapes and looks for spaces and people that can liberate her so she can liberate people from the subjugation that colonialism creates. Bomba is real and forces people to see their truth and expose it. Bomba is beautiful because it's black. Bomba is Diaspora and energy personified in different shades of Black bodies. Bomba creates a "Cosa nostra", una negrura compartida, un amor colectivo. Bomba is proactive and has created an Afro-diasporic bond that when the drum calls, those who know will respond because "El que sabe, sabe". The drum still sends codes that we recognize in our DNA, and Bomba is that voice that calls us to be present, seen, felt.

Bomba is a mother who teaches us how to create tribes and cabildos to learn how to make sense of the madness of the world we live in and uplift each other. Bomba is my friend and a memory in movement. Bomba is black power, a power that modifies values and behaviors, so we need to be careful and check ourselves because Bomba is also shaped by the people who make it. Bomba is guidance and always takes me back to dance with my ancestros. Bomba is purposeful and reminds me to build a legacy. Bomba is reciprocity. I give her life as she fills mine, and we both change, finding new meanings and ways to express new purposes for old causes, as we both grow old in some places and are reborn in others. Bomba is a life journey, a dream, a dream that can happen when we are kids or an inner child's dream when, as adults, we stopped believing in them. I had one with her once, and since then, I've been learning what Bomba can be. I am looking forward to the new meanings and purposes of this muse in my life. And as long as drums beat, I shall dance and continue sharing this muse with others.

Part 4

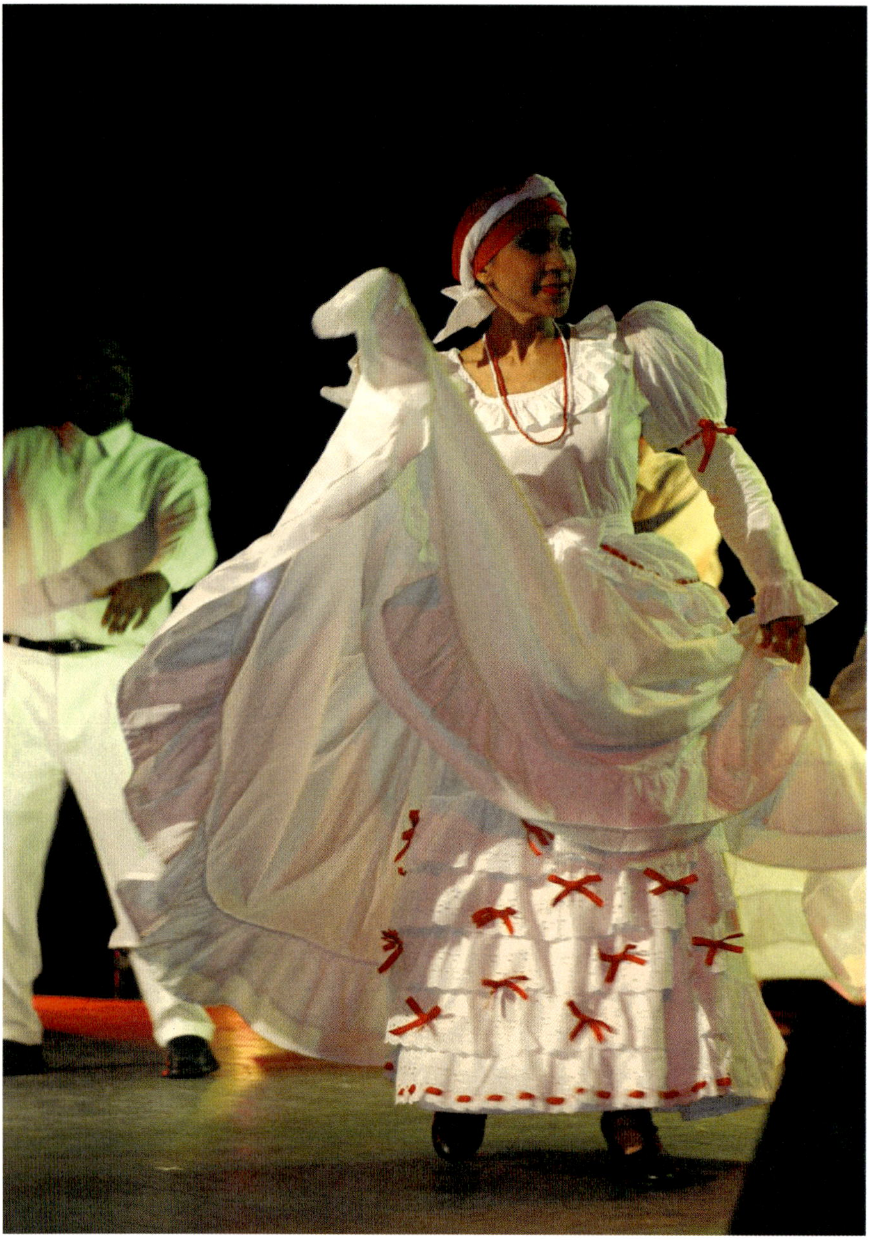

Peppermint candy dreams

"Dancing to the beat of a drum is magical"

I had a dream of peppermint enaguas under white skirts that were moved by beautiful, enchanting, black hands of women who called my spirit. I dreamt with my eyes open while the whiteness of their skirts created a light that covered me. Energy escaped my body, flying high to heaven in the middle of a park that rested between waters. Echoes of people singing, a breeze, and the sun's warmth created a feeling of freedom, innocence, and safety that only a good mother and a loving family can give. Bomba, like Pygmalion, asked me to give her life, and so I did.

Children like to daydream and believe in magic. They are curious and believe that anything is possible. I was a child who always felt total assurance that sooner or later I would have whatever I desired, and I cannot explain why. Like other kids, I was also told not to do this or that for my protection, but like all kids, I also ended up doing what I wasn't supposed to and got in trouble. Later in life, I learned that the powerful feeling of reassurance I felt was called faith, or like some say, the power of attraction. In my mind it was just plain old magic, and magic was always more powerful than my parents' No's.

The idea of dreaming had to do with being born in a land where everyone had one. I was surrounded by people who spoke about it, and it echoed everywhere. I too wanted a dream, and a cause without knowing I was already born with one. I was born in the land of the American dream, where Martin Luther King Jr.'s voice vibrated in the air and I too heard it even after his death. His dream was a nightmare for white folks, and for everyone else it was a reason to continue fighting for what they believed in. Some of these dreams were about freedom and equality, and for others about wealth and how to keep it, but while we were dreaming and surviving, white people were living. I believed that dreams came true because my parents taught me, and they did but not only with faith. They worked hard and had perseverance. They left Puerto Rico in search of something. I was born in a city where anything was possible, created, sold, and bought; even people. In that same city, I was conditioned in school to forget what I learned at home and was almost brainwashed with stories about living in the home of the brave and the land of the free. A land where violence is needed to survive, where we should be proud of who we are and defend where we stand, as if we stood on something that belonged to us. A nation that had four greedy fathers that people wrote songs about. We all pledged to an allegiance half asleep and cold, without knowing our "fathers" did not recognize or claim us. We just sang and regurgitated lies until they made sure we believed them. I sang the anthem every morning and pledged allegiance to a flag that did not care for me unless I gave something back. We all sang out of the top of our lungs the part that says; the land of the free! without thinking we would have to pay a higher price for ours.

NYC, an awesome place where most people do not own anything, especially in The Bronx. Back then was even worse because a rental could end up in flames. Although New York City is a place of opportunities and abundance, it is a place that is always testing people to see who makes it and who breaks in the process. It forces people to survive without being in the present because it constantly reminds people of the past. In this city the past is a lucrative business. The past means therapy, triggers, boundaries, stereotypes, fear, control, and keeping history intact. For my family, the past was a real West Side Story. At some point the West Side was the setting for many Marias and Ricardos who wanted or had to live in America. Gangs and turfs were real, and all of that meant defending and representing their identity. Some of the elders in my family had already migrated in the '40s and '50s and brought others with them. We were a big family back then, and while many moved to New York City, others stayed in Puerto Rico living their dream of the possibility of independence and defending a very peculiar identity of a criollo jibaro, criollo negro, creole X in a modern version of Los Tiempos de la Colonia. For Puerto Ricans in NYC was hard. It was living una realidad alterna that left everyone a bit lost between two worlds, ni allá, ni acá, because Nuyoricans do not really fit anywhere, and we are forced to create our universe, our space. I grew up moving between New York City and Puerto Rico. I lived in a Puerto Rico my parents built for me in The Bronx, and later a New York City I created for myself in Puerto Rico. Places where the most important common denominator for me was love. Love for my family, the land, and for the cultures that I identified with.

I remember that as much as my parents liked New York, they wanted to return to Puerto Rico, so they bought a house in the town of Carolina. In those travels, I often felt I had to choose to be one thing or the other, to be from one place or another, so eventually I learned to create my own spaces, and identity. When I was around six, I built my own place with a box where my mother's washing machine came in, in my parent's apartment. I had a little rug and toys in there, and my mom made a window for me and everything. It was fun and cozy. I was an only child at the time. I was also building my identity with all the information that my parents, society, media, school, NY, and Puerto Rico had input in me. When school was over, my parents used to check the house and visit the family in Puerto Rico, trying to find the right time to stay and settle. In my box, my space, I dreamt of being "grande" but was not sure where I was going to end up being.

A year or two later, on one of our trips to the island, my mother took me to a park in Old San Juan. It was a sunny afternoon, and my mother took me to Luis Muñoz Rivera Park. I remember it was a beautiful day, but also humid and hot. A playful breeze alleviated the sting on my skin from the unmerciful sun. An immense, deep blue sky was over us like a tent, and because NYC skies are usually gray, it was hard not to gaze at such a colorful site.

A lot of kids ran and screamed chasing each other, while others played with their toys, and parents awaited the swings for their kids while others physically fought for them. I finally had the chance to get on one of them, and I swung high as if I was flying, going higher each time. As I flew higher, the wind gave me the aroma of the ocean, and it was so strong that I could taste the saltiness. The breeze also brought sounds from afar. Deep sounds called me and made my mom, and everyone else in the park wonder where they came from. I slowly stopped swinging until I made a full stop, and I paid attention to what I was hearing. I had never heard those sounds before. I looked around, and people began to walk toward the place where they came from. My mother and I started walking, and I remember that when we got there, I saw a group of people dressed in a very peculiar way.

The women had their heads wrapped and their dresses really impressed me. They looked stunning, as if they had time traveled from the past and somehow appeared in the middle of the park. I had only seen people dressed like that in paintings, and maybe on television. Some looked very young, and there was a man who seemed to be the leader. He was a black man with a friendly face. I was captivated by the ladies' dresses, the musical instruments, the suspense. I knew that something special was going to happen. Suddenly, they started playing the drums again, and there, right in front of me, I heard the sounds that were missing from my grandmother's stories and that she tried emulating as she danced for me. I heard the word Bomba again, and I understood that the music I was hearing belonged to my grandmother's memories. The universe gave me the opportunity to see the images my grandmother kept telling me about and cherished. I saw images that belonged to her childhood. When they began dancing, I saw a classic scene that captivated my senses.

It was a magical moment for me. It was love at first sight and sound. I fell in love with Bomba when I was a kid. I heard it, I saw it, and I felt it in my heart. The women's dresses looked as if they had a life of their own. The dancers moved them as gracefully as they could, even though they struggled at times because the wind wanted to dance with them too. That dynamic went on for a while until everything synchronized. A calmness suddenly happened as if those drumming sounds sent a message to Mother Nature, and the wind calmed and turned into a smooth caressing breeze. No efforts were made, and the skirts gave in. Both, the dancers and the slow breeze embraced one another and made the fabric look like wings. I remember the beat of the drums saying something to my soul as my grandmother's dance did. The women wore decorated underskirts that displayed a rainbow of ribbons that stood out like candy. They smiled and seemed to have a conversation that only they knew what was going on. The man I saw in the park was Don Rafael Cepeda Atiles. His sons and daughters accompanied him. Chants accompanied the drums, some words were in Spanish while others in a language I did not understand, but everything felt right to me.

I wanted to be there with them. I wanted to dance and feel the drum near me. I remember my heart racing in my little body, and something happened to me. Bomba did something to me that was so intense that it followed me until I was able to meet her, feel her closely, and know her. After a while, they began to play a different rhythm. The dancers moved in a way that seemed more solemn. It felt weird because it was slower. Suddenly it got warmer, and the humidity intensified making it difficult to breathe. The music was like a heartbeat. The sun hid behind a cloud that felt like an umbrella, and I felt the drums' vibrations rumble in my chest and stomach. I felt as if something huge was over me. Even though I was there, I felt separated from everything else. I felt that there was an energy around me. I took a deep breath and I said I wanted that. I wanted to dance to that music. There was no abracadabra, just simple words filled with intention and envisioning myself dressed like the ladies in the group. For some reason I didn't want my mother to know what I had wished for. I knew we were going back to New York, so I guess I didn't want her to remind me and mess up my wish with reason.

I visualized myself dressed in the same outfit the ladies wore. I chose the underskirt with the red ribbons. I saw myself with my peppermint underskirt, and my red headwrap while standing with them. I felt chills all over and knew there was something special between Bomba and I. Bomba enchanted me and has not let me go since then. That day maybe destiny showed me part of my future or perhaps I designed it then and there with my soul. Either way, it was magical. As if my guardian angel and Oya Yansa snatched the vibrations that came out of my mouth, and lifted them as high as they could to Olodumare. I remember I told my grandmother what I had seen and she smiled. I knew something would happen after that day, I guess she knew too; I just had to be very patient. My wish did not come true during my childhood due to many things, including our travels. Eventually, after many years I became that vision of a Bomba dancer wearing a peppermint underskirt. I still look at the park between waters covered by a deep blue tent, and wonder how many prayers and wishes have been made there and come true. I am grateful that my peppermint dream manifested, and that it has refreshed my life's journey to this day. Bomba has brought me many joys and valuable lessons. Some of those lessons have to do with words, my grandmother moving, and the people I have met throughout my life that have planted a rare seed in my heart and that grew into a tree. My elders have taught me how to take care of it and share its shade with others. Just like a Bomba song says: "Estoy buscando un árbol que me de sombra". This chorus means I am looking for a tree that can give me shade, a tree that can refresh me. My grandmother and other elders, my parents, and special people that have become my extended family have been that tree for me. Its shade has refreshed my imagination and lifted my spirit when I have felt I've needed support. That tree represents many things, including a special place where my soul finds peace, and where I meet with people I love. Under the shade of that tree, I also ground myself, and create my utopia.

I still believe in magic to create extraordinary things. I still believe in flying and dreaming about things that make my heart rush with wonder. I believe in words that conjure wishes and design purposes, words that float high and reach the ears of those who can make them come true. Now and then, I still go to parks looking for a swing, and when I find one, I smile as I go higher and higher.

Modupué Baba mi Kabiesí, Shangó and Oyá Yanza

Part 5

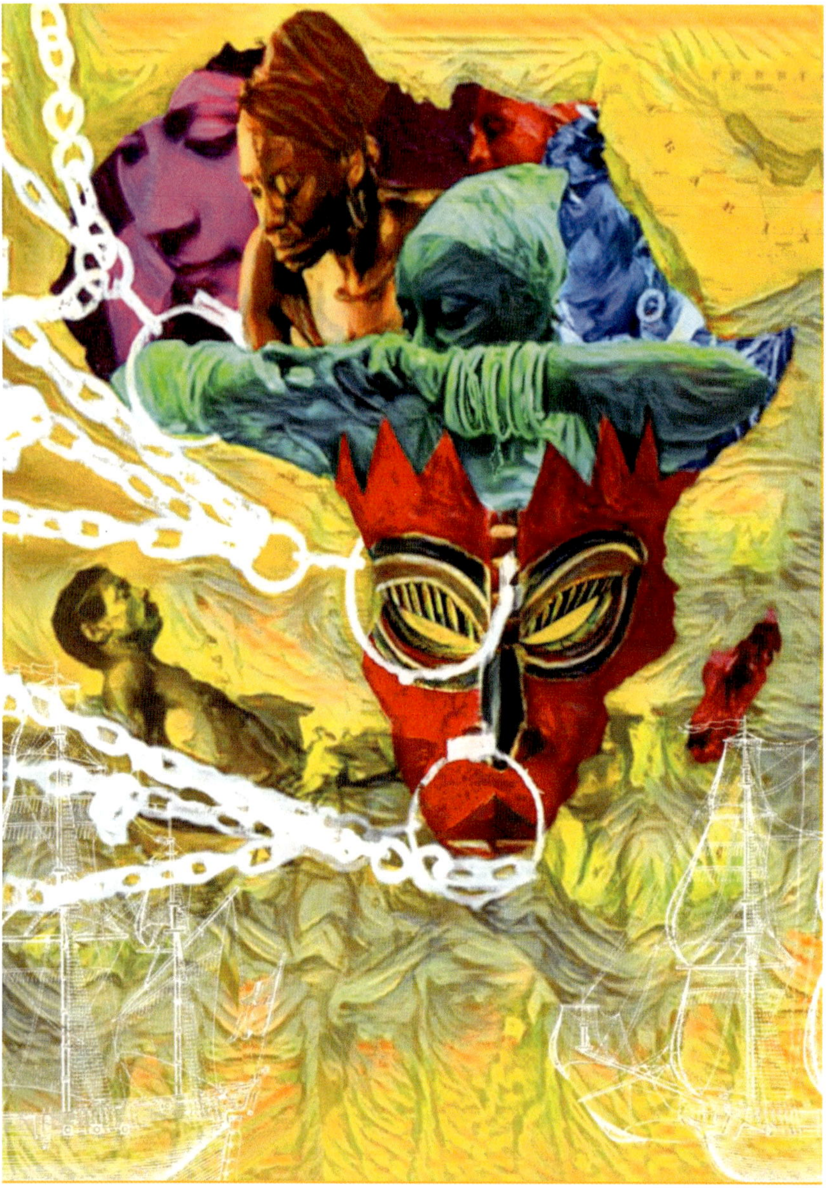

A muse called Puerto Africa

When space does not exist, it needs to be created

When in Rome, do as Romans do; when in New York, do as New Yorkers do; when in Puerto Rico, do as Puerto Ricans do; and when there is no space for you to go to, create it and do as you please. We need spaces to create paradise even if with time they turn into hell, but the important thing is to manifest what lives in the imagination. We become, learn, and grow in places that change and change us. The arts build those experiences and places where reality is not absolute and the stage is key in the creation of these multiple truths.

Bomba traveled from plantations to the homes of a few families, from there to the streets, and ended up on a stage. It was this platform that opened the door for Bomba's visibility, the education about its existence, and its history for the benefit of other generations. It became a Puerto Rican folkloric art that was performed in the island and became transnational. The stage has also made people notice black performers or lack of black representation in Bomba. Bomba revived and transformed our African cultural heritage into a performing art that also reached the media. This practical way of teaching Puerto Rican black history through music and dance as entertainment reached younger generations. Bomba, una cosa de negros, that was once devalued, ignored, and controversial became art thanks to the hard work of a few Puerto Rican black families, and the stage was the incubator where Bomba began evolving into the phenomenon that is today.

The importance of this resurgence of Bomba in Puerto Rico was mainly because there was, and unfortunately continues to be an intentional political agenda of removing black people from our national stories, and having a Puerto Rico without Puerto Ricans, especially the black ones. There has not been any real concern about educating on the valuable contributions of black people in Puerto Rico's history. The fact is that the agenda was to destroy any ideas that defined what means to be Puerto Rican, alongside with the ideas of independence, patriotism, national identity, and our symbols, as a product of colonization. Before the 60s, there was a time when Puerto Rican identity became a threat and a target, and with that, Bomba almost vanished from the collective memory of Puerto Rican people. The Gag Law, Ley de Mordaza, is an example of those attempts to erase our identity for political and economic purposes. North American culture, customs, and values influenced Puerto Rican identity, and even though countercultural movements were happening simultaneously, young people were easier to condition, and prone to assimilate without any resistance a gringo culture that made their way through fashion, dance, and music, and a false sense of power that came with the English language, and a privileged attitude that also had to do with the color of the skin. I was aware of how trends influenced me and how people in Puerto Rico talked about New York City, and about Puerto Ricans made in NYC, especially urban Puerto Ricans who were always checking out what was coming from afuera. "De afuera" became the phrase that was used to refer to people and things that came from the United States.

I believe that politics made the stage a powerful place to voice what was going on in a way that only the arts can. Art can disguise things and make ugly truths look pretty. Music and dance can lead a nation into a revolution, and visual arts can depict the flaws of a society or create the possibility of a better one. Artists used the stage to do things their way. They denounced the status quo, and challenged the system even when the audience did not comprehend their work and criticized their art, because some of these artists were ahead of their time and very misunderstood.

During the '70s I was a child growing up with a bicultural consciousness, and as I look back, I see how all of those experiences shaped my worldview. I grew up in a constant process of interculturalism. I witnessed a Pan-African movement that was exercised differently depending on where I was. Of course, I did not know these concepts back then, but I could describe what was happening around me, to me, and compare those experiences with the references I had, and reflect on how that affected me. Unfortunately, the narratives have not changed that much. Black people, their history, conditions, cultures, religions, and everything African or descendant from it, including the body of black people, are profitable and bonded to a system that hates black people but does not want, and cannot let them go either. White people made a business out of black people, and have also profited on their traumas. The sad truth is that slavery evolved into this modern-day society where everyone is enslaved. Black, brown, and also white people, that live stressed out with fear, because karma is a bitch, are also colonized. They have privileges, no doubt about that, but their ancestor's sins stare at them every day, all day, at least in NYC, and they cannot escape from that either, so we are all trapped in this sweet hell of prosperity and dreams. The situation is so obvious that books have been written about the new Jim Crow, but nobody wants to solve the situation because we all know that Uncle Sam, and this government does not give two craps for its people, especially who they call minorities, and they have the military ready to remind us all of who is boss. Since life is precious to all, and most of all to the enslaved, while things get sorted out, some pray, others work and protest, others do art and imagine better days, some use drugs while others go crazy, and we all wait for a holy or alien rapture to happen.

Back to my memorias, while growing up in New York, I remember hearing news and conversations about civil rights to improve the quality of life for black people, and that included Puerto Ricans. In Puerto Rico, I heard my family talking about Puerto Rico's independence, and a black movement that echoed what was happening in Cuba, and other places in the Caribbean. This rise of Puerto Rican black people, the consciousness of social justice, and black identity was spearheaded by artists who were trying to create a collective consciousness about these ideas by using poetry, music, dance, traditions, and culture as creative catalysts. Puerto Rican black artists such as Juan Boria, Harry Rexach, and Sylvia del Villard, to mention a few, were breaking the rules, and taking these opportunities that were limited at the time. Bomba groups like The Cepeda Family from Santurce, and the Ayala Family from Loiza were also becoming renown, and eventually became what today we call Instituciones Folklóricas.

There were many college students and educators who joined the movement, and became the voices of a young black Puerto Rican generation who needed, and wanted a better future for themselves. My aunt, Iris L. Medina, was an educator, and an advocate for the movement. The things I heard of and saw were responses to a racial and socio-political problem that needed to be addressed, and the people that suffered the most were Afro Puerto Ricans, that back then were not identifying themselves with that term. What was happening in Puerto Rico was a complete denial of the existence of racism and oppression of the US. The system chose to play it safe for the sake of the colony, and the dollar created a culture of ignorance and denial. It was easier to not speak or educate on the matter, it was better to become color-blind while a racist and patriarchal system continued developing, and conditioning the minds of the majority of Puerto Ricans. The subliminal message seemed to be that it was better to blend in into invisibility rather than to stand out, and the color of the skin determined the fate of many.

On one of those trips in "La guagua aerea", my aunts wanted to go to Las fiestas de Loiza, that are the feast of Santiago Apostol. Loiza is a beautiful town. A very traditional place known for its black demographic. Las Fiestas de Santiago Apostol is one of the traditions that are celebrated annually during the month of July, which later became Las Fiestas de Loiza for short. I remember the town being crowded, and as we drove by, I noticed how familiar people were. Everyone knew each other, or so it seemed. That is how Puerto Ricans usually are; sociable, parlanchines, alegres y dadivosos.

People shared smiles, conversations, and were having a good time. We walked on dirt roads that were packed with people, and the smell of burnt wood filled the air. A particular memory came to me as I was writing that made me reflect on a quote from Maya Angelou: *"People live in direct relation to the heroes and the sheroes that they have."* I agree with her. I had the pleasure to have met a few of them, and I did in that visit to Loiza.

The patron's feast is a beautiful carnival where syncretism is celebrated. As a part of the celebration there are processions and misas in the church because it was meant to have a religious purpose, and was not only for entertainment. There are costume competitions, a queen is chosen to represent the town, and other activities. La Loca, el Vejigante, el Caballero, are some of the main characters of this celebration where the past comes to life, and the ancestors join the living. I remember being in the middle of a pitiless humidity that made everyone break a sweat without even moving.

The smells of smoked food like empanadas de jueyes, coconut arepas and food cooked in the Buren teased me. These are some of the traditional foods cooked on a metal plank heated with woodfire that people love. They cook alcapurrias de jueyes or ground beef with a Boricua sazón that is incomparable. These fried foods are really tasty, crispy on the outside, and tender inside with flavorful fillings that are part of Loiza's cuisine. The raw masas that are put on a uva playera leaf to shape it, and then placed in hot oil to fry to a crisp are delicious! The rice with crab and coconut they cook is covered with plantain leaves, which add a delicious taste to it, and people make long lines to feast on these wonderful African rooted delicacies.

While we walked, the music played loud and my aunts bumped into people they knew. We stood near a tall stage where only musical instruments decorated the scene. The stage has always caught my attention. There is something about it that still makes my heart pound hard. It is not really about wanting to be on it, but rather the suspense, the wait, and possibilities of what can happen there that fills me with excitement. The stage is where history can be recreated, created, and interpreted. It produces images that become engraved in people's subconscious. It is also a multipurpose resource where arts and politics meet to resist, engage, revolutionize, explore, and fundamentally provoke a response. Like a magnet, the stage drew people in and lured us with its power. After a while, a few men got up on stage and began to set things up and organize their instruments that awaited passively. People stared at them, made comments that it was about time that somebody showed up, and finally, it seemed as if the show was going to start. The musicians wore dashikis and spoke among themselves. I have to admit that I was surprised to see them in those clothes. I used to see people wearing dashikis in New York City. It was the Afrocentric look of the time that became a fashion trend. African dashikis and Afros were part of the 70s look for black people, including Afro Boricuas in New York City. Slowly, Puerto Ricans were wearing a fashion that made a political and racial statement.

The musicians played for a few minutes to warm up and smiled as they built up their energy. Then suddenly, like a vision, a monument appeared. This stunning, tall, powerhouse woman came on stage and I could not take my eyes off her. Ms. Sylvia del Villard Moreno. I will never forget that first impression for as long as I live. She was proud, and there was something mystical about her. Her muscular body showed more than her physical strength. Her body affirmed her inner force and her black roots. She was determined to captivate the public and get her message across, not only with her voice, and gestures but through her whole body. The music created the sounds that helped create poetic images as she spoke, and recited her poetry. Her voice was firm, and the way she talked was precise, like an orator. Her poems were of those writers who described the Caribbean with rich descriptive words and onomatopoeia that helped you see what she was talking about. Luis Palés Matos and Fortunato Vizcarrondo were some of the poets who she admired. Her performing wardrobe was simple and revealing. I remember that her head was not wrapped. Her hair was in a small bun on the top of her head, and big hoop earrings adorned her face. She wore a lot of silver bracelets and other accessories that decorated her arms and neck. Her wardrobe consisted of a small top in African fabric, and a small skirt that left uncovered her long, muscular legs and thighs. She was barefooted, and each step was firm and left a legacy. She did not smile, and I knew she was not there to play around. She reminded me of my mother, my grandmother, and her sisters. There was something about Sylvia's character and attitude that was familiar. Sylvia del Villard was regal. She had other dancers that accompanied her who wore similar clothing but not like hers. For some reason, her presence was so strong that even though I knew there were other dancers with her, I could not notice them because she was the center of everyone's attention, even if it was for different reasons.

She recited and I was mesmerized by her power. I remember that while that beautiful woman was on stage sharing her blackness, her pride, and soul, something was happening around me and in front of her. Murmurs here and there criticized her looks and mocked her. The ignorance of people that some were probably drunk, conditioned, and others just plain disrespectful made me sad. I was heartbroken for her. We say in Spanish: "Me dió verguenza ajena." Before me, standing tall and probably nervous too, was an artist ahead of her time, giving her all, and some were not realizing the powerful message she was sending them, not necessarily in her poetry, but with her presence, and most of all her body. The reason why I mention the body is because there is a huge importance of what the female black body represents. It was the first time I saw someone representing so many things with only her presence. I was upset because people around me were making it difficult for me to enjoy the performance. It had to take a lot of courage to do what she did back then. I didn't know the significance of her work until I grew up, but even a child knows when a person has authority, and because I saw the women in my family in her, I guess that moment became personal. What her presence said to me was: We are here, our ancestors are here, I am here. Whether you like it or not, whether you understand me or not, and I am you.

That memory faded a bit but never went away. It made me think about the complexities of reconciling all the elements that make up our identity. Sylvia studied in Tennessee during Jim Crow, and only she knew the racist experiences she had to endure that transformed her, and her art into a social mission and a political activist. She was a feminist who set her flag with her art. Her body was her platform. As a black woman her presence alone was already a political act of resistance in the liberated way, she chose to represent herself. Her political ideas, and artistry were not appreciated enough or acknowledged enough in Puerto Rico. I am sure that her character must have been strong, and like all black people, when we do things, there is sometimes a background of trauma, disadvantage, and many other issues that can complicate things, but despite all of that, the work needs to be done, and gets done. Her flaws, whatever they might have been, cannot erase the significance of her work. It should not be forgotten, and now that there seem to be a" Black is Back" movement in Puerto Rico, Sylvia's work should be considered, not only in the arts, but also in academia.

People sometimes conform to certain circumstances as a result of being tired of a long history of struggles, oppression, and generational woundings. Sylvia del Villard Moreno represented Santurce, Loiza, New York City, and every black town, and every black woman in Puerto Rico, Tennessee, and the United States. It must have been painful for her to see her people dismissing her in her land, and taking for granted what she was giving them with so much dedication and passion. That memory stood with me and now I can understand her. That was another moment where the arts changed my life. Even as a child in New York City I knew how it felt to be misunderstood or defined in a way that did not represent me. That day I witnessed black people condemning a black artist for doing black art to empower them. Sylvia del Villard had to struggle with all the institutionalized racism that existed at the time to leave an artistic and political legacy for future generations, or at least for me.

That encounter with her made me think about how shallow and brainwashed society can be. Sylvia chose to represent herself in an honest and controversial way. She embraced her blackness in all its forms, and challenged the notions that set the standards of beauty by recreating an authentic image, which was very different from the colonized aesthetic presented on stage by the Bomba families who performed at the time. Sylvia was a representation of our enslaved ancestors, but not from a position of defeat. She became a visual representation of them in the way they might have been before they were enslaved.

Sylvia's work taught me that artist's stories should be told because someone, somewhere, is listening. That woman claimed her negritude instead of denying it. Her gestural language showed passion and Sylvia stood by her truth. Even though that truth had been censored by her Puerto Rican brothers and sisters, she became a political agency that focused on feminism and black identity. Sylvia dealt with the controversies that her presence caused. She wanted to teach her people about what was happening in the belly of the United States. She wanted to teach about Africanness and she was woke enough to do the job. Sylvia del Villard knew Jim Crow hid in Puerto Rico's coasts behind laws and politicians. She knew that bastard was becoming a "criollo" and was creeping into the minds of Puerto Ricans that were already acclimated to oppression. Sylvia returned to Puerto Rico on a mission of emancipating younger generations and liberating her people from mental slavery. She created a new image, an Afro Puerto Rican one. Sylvia used all the platforms she could to blow the lid off racism, and how it was manipulating the politics that affected black artists. Denunció the lack of equality and equity in Puerto Rican black communities because she was living it. That memory crystallized in me, and years later she came to life to push me to do the same and give her a voice. Her spirit missed the stage, and years later she was mentioned, remembered, and honored.

Going back to that afternoon in the fiestas, after her performance, Mr. Juan Boria also shared a few poems by the same poets. Meanwhile, in Cuba, Nicolas Guillen was doing his artistic and political work, and in the United States, the Black Panthers and The Young Lords in NYC were shaking the foundation that had black people, African Americans, and Puerto Ricans stuck in poverty and rubble. People tend to digest lighter food better, so metaphorically speaking, I guess Juan Boria's performance was easier to process by the masses. Everybody's work was part of a movement of resistance and it was every artist's right to express their talents in the ways they understood was best. He was very charismatic. He was a very thin man with wide, round eyes who made exaggerated gestures while he recited poems about black children, black women, dark places, and black problems. After Mr. Boria did his part, there was a short break, and another group came on stage that reminded me of the group I saw in the park where I had my peppermint dream. They were La Familia Ayala.

The men looked very elegant, but I noticed that all the dancers were barefooted. Their dancing style was very different. Hips moved from side to side without restrictions. It was like the women's bodies wanted to break loose from all the fabric that concealed it, which made the looked as if they were forced to wear the dresses. The dresses, unlike the Cepedas, were not the focus of attention. What I remember was the footwork and hips moving that stayed on the beat. Their arms moved synchronized with hips that danced along to a different rhythm that I had not heard before. Both men and women moved their bodies in a flirtatious way, and the energy was different. The looks on their faces when couples danced had a picardía that was contagious.

The men looked at the women's hips shaking and opened their arms and eyes as if they were ready to catch their butt in case it detached. Their choreographies were very dynamic, and dancers on and off stage went into a frenzy. I noticed how the audience enjoyed it. Their performance did not put any pressure on the people there; they just made it fun. There was nothing to analyze, nothing that made people feel discomfort or the need to reflect on. Nobody stood still. Everyone danced with them and sang the coros, while some men enjoyed the commotion and the shaking hips and round, big asses around them. In the middle of all of that, I stood still. I didn't know what I felt because it was a discombobulated moment that didn't make sense to me. The Bomba performance became a safer way to create a collective narrative that was less intense than Sylvia's, but I'll never forget her.

The party was not over, but we had to leave. I left with many unanswered questions and mixed feelings that time has helped me understand and answer. I guess I left thinking about my idea of New York Black Power vis a vis Puerto Rican Black Power. The information contained in these memories continue to change as I do with time, but what has remained is the impact of the presence of the body on stage. All the information that a body holds and gives, even before it starts performing is powerful. The fact that Sylvia's performance provoked a cultural shock was not surprising at all. The movements of her dance were different, her look was different, and the feeling of it all was new. Sylvia del Villard's work was a remembrance of a painful past that people refuse to deal with because it was a part of the present. Sylvia refused to be gagged. She refused to negotiate with her blackness and her art, which made her work very difficult. Once again, the skin marked a destiny that did not let her complete her projects without struggles and frustrations in her own country. She passed away with an unfinished dream. The name of that project was Puerto Africa. I would have loved to see it, but since that was not possible and I believe in magic, something magical eventually happened.

In 2006, I started collaborating with two artists who were building a Bomba community in California. They became important people in the development of a Bomba movement in The Bay area. These cultural collaborators took the Bay by storm. Ms. Cynthia Renta and Denis Solis created an Afro-Puerto Rican proposal that opened a door for people there to learn Bomba, but most importantly, to teach them a part of our history through music and dance. They focused their work on teaching about an Afro-Puerto Rican history that people became obsessed with. Although the work had already happened in NYC and Puerto Rico, they too became part of a women's movement that enabled a transnational exchange of artists that empowered women with a musical project that left a legacy as well. Cynthia Renta brought her Jersey/Ricanness and mixed it with Denis Solis's Mexican roots, and passion for Bomba music, and both of them accomplished their mission.

In my opinion, what made things take off successfully in The Bay, was their commitment and determination to see their dreams come true. The energy that peoples put into things, and their intentions is the foundation of all great things. It was a time when people, time, and intentions synchronized. I had the privilege of being invited to partake in that process, and assist in a few artistic productions where Bomba was the main attraction and brought women together.

In 2006, we did *Un camino por el cañaveral.* La Peña Cultural Center in Berkley was the spot where we produced the first women's Bomba ensemble performance. Guests from NYC, and Puerto Rico were part of this performance. After that show, and evaluating the event, we were ready for the next thing. Cynthia and I shared a cup of coffee in a Café, and discussed different ideas to choose what the content of the next show would be. Women were the focus of our next project's theme. Puerto Rican historical women became the muses and protagonists of the next proposal. *Cimarronaje* was the name of that powerful show that took place in the year 2008. Guests from Chicago, Puerto Rico, other parts of California, and New York City participated in the event. In 2017 I heard that the same concept was done by other artists in Puerto Rico who had coincidentally participated as guests in the original show in California. This made me think about how powerful that show was, and how it marked others to inspire them to repeat it.

It is interesting to see how the spirits of the dead, the work of the living, and collective ideas can create something so inspiring. The proposition for this particular show was that each independent artistic piece was going to be a homage to a Puerto Rican woman who had contributed to our history. The artist had to choose which Puerto Rican woman they wanted to represent, and create a piece with Bomba music as a foundation for their piece. Everything was original, from the music, theatrical concept, and dance. After we organized the ideas I returned to Puerto Rico, but I did not know who I was going to choose. I did not have any particular person in mind at the time. I was too busy back then because I had a double life, you see. I was a school teacher during the day, and an artist, and producer after 3:00 p.m.

I trusted that at some point I was going to come up with an idea to produce the piece. A veces a mi me pasan cosas extrañas y dejo que fluyan. A veces me sorprenden y otras veces no, pero sé que todo tiene su propósito.

One night, I came home from work. I was performing somewhere and was super tired. I wasn't thinking about anything that wasn't getting home and resting. I remember waking up in the middle of the night because I dreamt of Sylvia del Villard. In my dream, she was in my bedroom, dancing in front of my closet mirror. It was so vivid that I woke up confused. I felt her presence and her energy as if she was really there. I went back to sleep, but when I woke up the next morning I remembered, and I knew that was a sign. That dream was the answer that I was looking for. Sylvia was my inspiration for the artistic piece that I was going to create. I was going to do an homage to Sylvia del Villard Moreno as a token of respect and appreciation for what she taught me without even knowing it, because I doubt that she saw me, or maybe she did.

When I started doing my research, I thought that perhaps Sylvia's power, and strong personality hid fear and anger because of what she experienced while she was in the United States. Perhaps she hid the fact that she was vulnerable or felt unappreciated. She knew the racist America that others had not seen. She saw the brutality and duality of the land that trapped us, and how the Constitution was never meant to be enjoyed by the people of the United States that had her skin color. It must have been terrible to feel alone in her own country, and still have hopes for something better for herself, her family, and fellow Puerto Ricans. Sylvia learned how racism dissects black people, especially women. I think that when she went to New York City, she felt hopeful, and the arts gave her a voice but did not ease her struggles. Her story talks about affiliations with Africans and African Americans that helped her have a clearer vision of her personal and artistic identity and mission. All of those lessons helped her find her way. All of those things helped me have a clearer vision of my creative plan and have my own idea about her as a woman and artist. My challenge was to know how to represent her without forgetting to be me.

Ultimately, what I learned in Loiza was that all of the performances that I saw spoke about the evolution of our history. All of those expressions made people feel something and came from a place of individual freedom. The freedom that allows an artist to choose how they want to do things and share themselves with the rest of the world. Even when wearing a costume, there is something special happening that is liberating and inspiring.

The message of freedom is in the movement, whether dancing, reciting, singing, or walking to and from a stage or stage in life. The message is to know how to create freedom for ourselves no matter where we are or the circumstances. Sylvia resisted, but in this case, I needed to submit and let her guide me, not so much in movement but in the message that she wanted to give me. I interpreted in that dream that she wanted to be remembered and use my voice.

I wrote Puerto Africa, a spoken word piece that closed *Cimarronaje* and ended with Sylvia's image on stage as an homage and probably closure to a project se never did. Sylvia del Villard became my sheroe. She taught me the price that must be paid to do what you believe in. I learned that even if others censor your artistry, there is great power in authenticity that is worth every struggle, and the cause is greater than the challenges.

Puerto Africa, the name of her unfinished project and how I named my piece for the show, was a mix of poetry, Bomba music, and Hip Hop because these things represented me. I invited the artist Awilda Sterling, one of Sylvia's former students, dancer and visual artist, to collaborate with me. The piece opened with Ms. Sterling doing a silent piece called *Un Camino en el Rio*, where she entered with ankle bracelets that made natural sounds to create the illusion of the Yoruba deity, Oshun, walking by the river. Her exit was my cue, and as she left the stage with the audience's attention, and a Hip Hop beat, Sylvia and I occupied the stage.

The piece ended with a Yubá. The Bomba rhythm that I heard when I was a little girl in the park in Old San Juan. Cimarronaje ended with the presence of all the guest artists entering the stage while chanting Puerto Africa. They sang for Sylvia, for Africa and Puerto Rico. The artists came onto the stage, and the collective voices joined to create a force. I recited, sang, and danced. Sylvia was there and her image in the backdrop was majestic. To my surprise, Sylvia del Villard Moreno was the only dark-skinned woman amongst all the Puerto Rican women who were chosen to be represented. Sylvia was there and I was satisfied. I ended the piece facing her with my fist up in remembrance of her resistance, her mission to abolish racism, the freedom she claimed with her body, and be seen for who she was—a powerful woman, a Sheroe.

I honored the fact that she became a voice for her people. I feel that her homage revived her name in the memories of many. After that event, I was asked to perform it in 2015 for the New York Puerto Rican Parade, which was dedicated to Afro-Puerto Rican culture. Suddenly, interviews and memories of her work regained importance. I was happy for her and hope her spirit continues evolving into light, peace, and, most of all, the minds of those who claim their blackness.

Puerto Africa

Poema dedicado a Sylvia del Villard

My blackness has been censured
Lastimada, desfigurada
ultrajada, negociada

Me recibieron tus garras abiertas
Abrazos que laceraron mi espalda
arrancándome las alas

Me regalaste perfume de salitre y flores de hierro
que entrelazastes entre mis manos

Manos que una vez fueron libres

En contra de mi voluntad
entregué mi cápsula húmeda
Tinta que deformó mis cuentos de amor
en depravados mitos de lujuria
Entrañas en venta para encargar al hijo ingrato.
¡Caribe!
Me niega, me reprocha y me reprime
Pero no puede olvidarme.

Dejé mi huella en conciencias putrefactas
mi reflejo en tierra nívea y estéril
Y a pesar de todo eso, camino como toda una reina,
aquí en Puerto Africa

Mis hijos me llaman.
Cómo
Sirvienta, bruja, bruta, pobre
Negra raíz de la raza humana

Madre y abuela de muchos blancos
que amamanté con mis pechos
Les dí mi esencia, nutriente africano
que fortalece el espíritu del guerrero

Como esclavas vivimos, como guerreras luchamos
como heroinas sobrevivimos,
aquí en Puerto Africa

Censura hipócrita
Devuélveme mi piel, devuélveme mi voz
mis dioses, mi baile
mi tempo y mi tambor

Golpes sonoros que llaman a miles negros
libres, esclavos, reyes y reinas del este, del oeste, del norte
de lo profundo
hasta llegar al oido de aquél, del primero

Aquél hecho de la tibieza y el marrón de la tierra
del aliento de Olodumaré
con destino tan oscuro como Eshu
Magnífico como el rayo
dulce como la Iyalode del río

Y mientras camino en tierra conquistada, tierra ajena
mientras camino en esta tierra que ahora es mía
entre recuerdos de ancestros que llaman

Escucho el eco de mi patria
escucho mi propia voz entre el eco de miles reinas que claman

Puerto Africa

There is no freedom without resistance; there is no freedom without oppressing others. There is no freedom without deconstructing your old self, old habits, and beliefs. There is always something that needs to be pinned down, terminated, or sacrificed for a new idea, or a new you to reborn. Like Sylvia, I also walk like a queen in this world. Why the hell not? I know that I am more than a womb-man, I am more than the definitions of what society and systems have given me. I am more than the skin that covers my body. I am an extension of a divine source that according to many cannot be explained. Sylvia knew, and despite it all she walked in the middle of all the Puerto Africa's she created with her work. I guess she looked around as she recited her poems wondering when will we stop resisting? When will black art be used for something other than fighting injustice, or creating a moment to bámbula the sorrows of our ancestors, and not think about our lamentos?

Until that time comes… When at war, do as warriors do.

Part 6

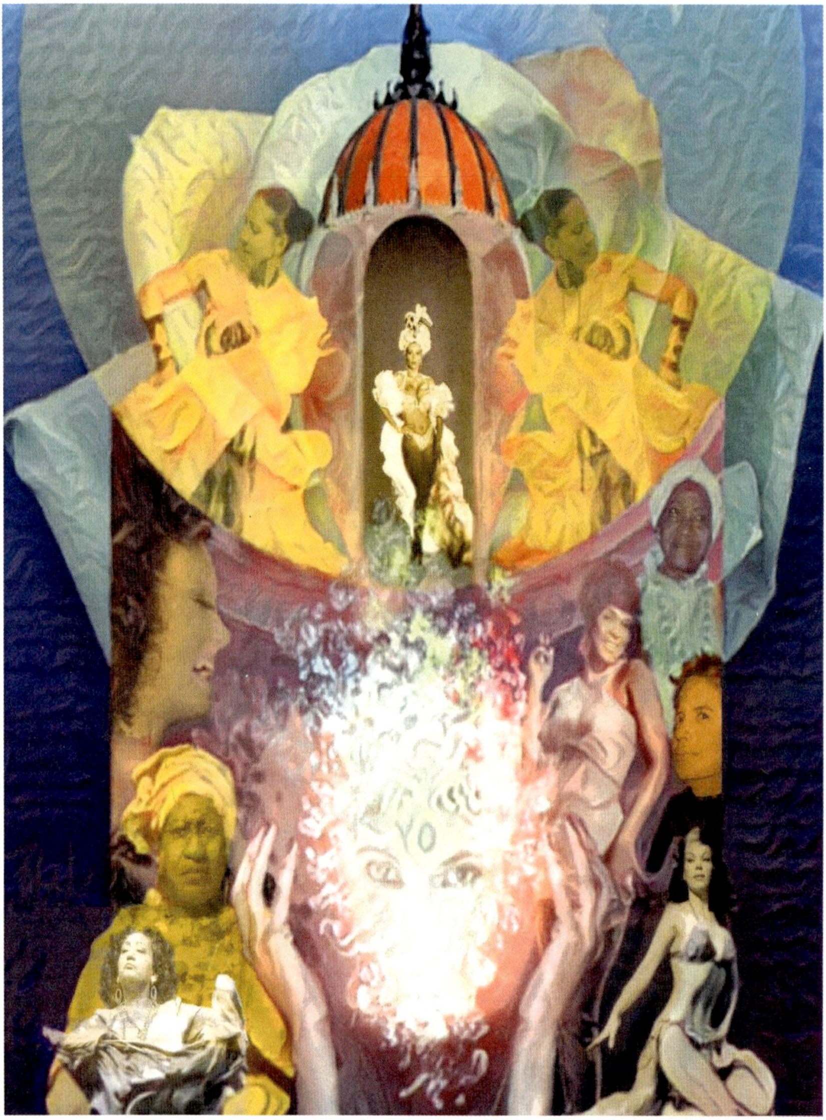

Musas Manifestadas

La historia en el cuerpo

Viva la resistance! The men and women that I have admired, my sheroes and heroes have used their bodies as a means of resistance. To resist we need to deal with discomfort, and making others uncomfortable too. The body as a subject, how it looks, and how it moves have been studied, and one of those purposes has been to be able to control it. Most of the time, body movements are judged based on subjective information that has been taught from early childhood and plays a part in the construction of how we perceive sexuality, race, and gender. The interpretation of the body and its movements, maintain a certain order in society, and anything that might disrupt that will be judged, and canceled. Needless to say, the dominant group, whether it is white people, men, or women in positions of power, will determine how and when changes to these interpretations can be made. Movements are inscribed with narratives that transform into something more than what they are. In dance, a black body is attached to a social class, historical misinformation, the prejudices that the system reinforces, and a myriad of information that does not allow the dancer to be a single being, or just a performer. Usually, black and brown people are subjected to the scrutiny of how others see their bodies and its usually tainted.

Bomba is important because it's the only conferment of Africa that, as a Puerto Rican woman, helps me understand the root that grounds me through movements and sounds. Bomba dance and music are some of the ancestral practices that have been imprinted in us as a means for survival. These so-called "primitive" patterns of sounds and movements, which is how Europeans described Bomba dance and music, help us to reconnect with ourselves, the environment, and with a higher power. Bomba is the dance of the oppressor and oppressed in the same body, and that is why Bomba can be very complicated.
The person who teaches should be aware of how we unconsciously, carry the oppressor's values in the body in form of shame that has been ingrained in us. Body shaming was used to control people,

especially women. The church and men have been supporters of controlling women's bodies, mostly black women's bodies. White women in positions of power have also played a role in this injustice. These issues have provoked the crippling of the body, and the ability to express itself naturally. Trauma contained in the body also changes how people move and react to the environment.

How black people move has been criticized, banned, and also imitated. One of the body movements that society has focused on the most, has been shaking, particularly when it is done by women. Shaking the body is one of those physical movements that release tension, and one that has been used often for Dance Therapy.

Before I learned to dance Bomba and the depths of this art form, I learned with a different Bomba how the shaking of the body can reshape the identity of a whole society. The Bomba that I am talking changed Puerto Rico. This Bomba was also personified in a woman's body that was not afraid of visibility and of using it to disrupt society's control over women's sexuality while also changing the concept of gender in Puerto Rico. This Bomba was Iris Chacón. But first, I must mention one of my grandmother's favorite dancers who appeared in Mexican films. A woman who made way for other vedettes, including Iris Chacón, and began to shake away the prejudice of an old-fashioned, rigid, and prudish society.

Latin America and the Caribbean had their share of avant-garde women, and their bodies revolutionized the standards imposed on their bodies and behavior. They changed tradition and unstabilized norms to change their roles, their voices, and their power in society. One of these musas was Yolanda Montes Farrington, also known as Tongolele. She was a pioneer. Ms. Montes, like Isadora Duncan, sought freedom in her dance and would not have it any other way. She was a vedette, and although she was not the only one in Mexico at the time, she was the one who gained the most fame. Tongolele was well-known in Puerto Rico because of the films she made. Yolanda Montes was born in the US, but her parents were Swedish and Spanish, and her grandmother on her mother's side was Tahitian. She was a beautiful woman who created a space for her independence in the arts, and according to her interviews, she cared more for her art than marriage. She was setting her own rules not only on the creative aspect of her life but also on what society expected from women in the late 1940s and 50s. I was familiar with her name because that is what some of my grandmother's friends called her because of a lunar de canas that she had from birth. I remember that Puerto Rican television always showed old, black-and-white films that created a weird connection to a past that my grandmother knew, and although it did not have to do with my time, I learned about the actors and music that my grandmother talked about because of these old movies.

Tongolele was a trendsetter and also a brave woman who used her art to change the movie industry, culture, and how others viewed the female body in movement. She combined Middle Eastern dance and Tahitian dance, mixed with some basic Western African dance movements that she learned in Cuba. Her dances were improvised, and she was the one to cue the drummers to change the beat instead of the other way around. Tongolele was sensual; her movements and beauty made her famous. What I find interesting about her career is the use of improvisation in all her dances, which gave her independence and control as a solo artist, which was not easy to have at the time. She empowered herself and broke with the era of militant art. Like Sylvia del Villard as a member of the Pan African movement of the time, Yolanda was part of the Generación de la Ruptura, which means the Rupture Generation. They defied the system and created their own rules. When I think about her dance movements, although they were critized, however, she was not and was supported by white men who wanted to sponsor her and put her in the spotlight because the color of her skin gave her that privilege. As I had mentioned previously, the connection between movement, sexuality, and the body that dance is a subject of scrutiny, but mostly when the body is black. I think that if the same dances that she did would have been performed by a black woman, the story would have been different, or perhaps there would not be a story at all. The leniency with Tongolele was because she was a white woman who looked exotic, and her skin color approved her pelvic movements. Her white pelvis was artistic and not vulgar or sexualized, as many would have viewed pelvic movements done by black women and men. Personally, the dances that I have seen in her movies needed more pep. Her performance seemed to lack strength, and even though she looked beautiful and did something daring at the time, I am sure a Cuban black dancer could have done a greater performance. I know the movements would have been executed better in response to the music. What I admire is how she owned her body and lived that truth through her art and politics, and how she changed the business that opened a door for other divas to follow in her footsteps.

Years later in Puerto Rico, a young woman from Puerto Nuevo became *La Bomba de Puerto Rico* and *La Vedette de América.* I got to see that Bomb on TV, in person, and I imitated her plenty of times while playing around as a kid with my cousin. Everybody was all up in her business. Her name: Iris Belia Chacón Tapia. Ms. Chacón was the real Puerto Rican Bomb. Way before Jennifer Lopez, Iris Chacón was that woman that people loved, admired, imitated, envied, and was also hated by other women. She sang, danced, acted, and was an entertainer. Iris Chacón had her first TV show during the 70s and 80s, which gave her a lot of international exposure. Those set of circumstances opened doors for her in the U.S. Iris was the woman with the *Coolant,* a term used to refer to her derriere, and she had a charm that won a North American audience that loved her, and if they did not, at least men loved her derriere. The term Coolant became popular due to a car oil commercial she did to advertise a brand that added to her acclaim and attention. Ms. Chacón not only showed ownership of her body like Tongolele, she also hired and befriended men as her backup dancers who were part of her entourage. These men were identified by society, as Gay men.

Looking back, Puerto Ricans were not ready to see the image of such a woman on TV. Those movements that shocked people the most was the unrestricted shaking of the body. Without a doubt, the movements of her buttocks and breasts made some people uncomfortable. There were concerns about how traditions imposed by patriarchal and religious beliefs were changing.

Criticisms were made based on the prerogatives of puritana housewives who thought her work was immoral. I guess people were struggling with the values of their times and were also resisting change. These traditions that we continue preserving and are also hidden behind folk art need to be evaluated now and then to ensure we are evolving. Meanwhile, Ms. Chacón was chasseing away her half-naked body through each show and changing the culture with the visibility of her curves, her butt, and also, which is very important, the presence of her dancers.

Iris Chacón spearheaded a movement for freedom and equality focused on dance performance, image, gender, spirituality, and sexuality. She was an advocate for a different society that was kept underground and oppressed. She created a space for herself and the artists who worked with her. Iris Chacón created a platform for male dancers who were only appreciated on stage and performing on TV. Her show's sets were very elegant and ahead of the times, sort of a Las Vegas kind of feel, and in that space, Iris placed dancing male black bodies on national TV, which began creating controversies.

Iris Chacón gambled with her future, and although for some, it might seem as if she had lost, the reality is that she won unimaginably. She took a risk and gave her dancers an opportunity for visibility, which would be very positive on one end and very complicated on the other for the people who resisted social change. Homosexuality was not tolerated. What we know now as the LGBTQIA community was kept a secret for the sake of social easement, an alleged national good morality, and to avoid harassment which ended at times in physical violence. It became difficult for people to choose what to criticize, whether her dance, her body, her dancers, or the media that piggybacked and made money from it all.

While that was happening, I was influenced by her dance and her boldness. I sang her songs and imitated her for fun, and that went on for a while until my early teens without understanding how this particular Bomba was changing my perception of my body in motion and place in society. I was learning about freedom and the freedom of others to be who they were publicly. I learned this because my cousin, Lucas Figueroa, was one of her dancers. He was talented and a beautiful human being. She gave him the opportunity to live his dream, and for that I will always be grateful to her.

The world knew about her work and also about the closet doors she opened to give the community visibility and the right to be free.

That freedom movement paved the way for gay people to create spaces where they felt they belonged. Gay clubs opened in Santurce, San Juan, and New York City, which was another important space for them. It was a time to uncover the body, gender, and the recognition that there were many identities in the societies we live in.

When Lucas and I were kids, we used to play together, and he would dress me up with tacos, comb my hair, and do my makeup like Iris Chacón. Most of the time he was the choreographer, and together we danced and did shows for my tías and other cousins who laughed at us and applauded us. He never dressed up as a woman, not even when we were older, or at least he never did in front of me. It was okay for him to be who he was sometimes because when his father was around, it was another story. Little did I know that by doing all of the things he did through play, he was visualizing his dreams, and once again having dreams is part of who we are and meant to do in this world. Sharing so closely with him helped me learn about the pain hidden behind his humor and laughter.

I learned about the hardship of gay people in society and how their image, movements, the presence of the body that physically defied la norma, unveiled a social hypocrisy that became threatening to straight men and also to some women who weren't so sure about the masculinity of their partners. Ms. Chacón broke the rules and broke a stiff society.

There was a certain look that her dancers had in common. They were fit because they were dancers, and also dressed in certain ways, and took care of their bodies, which later transformed into what we call a Metrosexual look. In the middle of that moral tornado, Iris Chacón kept dancing and acting. She was the center of attention in the center of tensions caused by a progressive era versus the conservative mentality of a Boricua society that examined everything that threatened their morality. Meanwhile, straight men and women used demeaning phrases to refer to her dancers. - "Mira esos maricones, los patos que bailan con Iris. A las locas se le van a salir las plumas", and other derogatory comments. They wanted to cancel a culture that created discomfort. The straights, the morals, created a very hostile environment that made it hard for homosexuals, but there was no going back to the closet.

While her show provided financial stability to her dancers and made a home for them, Broadway became that place in New York City that transformed theaters into safe spaces for homosexuals in the performing arts. The arts were forming a new perception and perspective about gender and movement. Iris shook her bootie to fame, and the more she danced, the more Puerto Rican men controlled their bodies to avoid giving the wrong impression. Women also changed. She set a new standard that made women more atrevidas. Women were reprogramming the way they saw themselves, and accentuating their natural, curvy Caribbean bodies with the fashion styles that helped. From the tight dresses, and the big hair, to the dark-eye lined eyes and moles that went with it, women changed their appearance. They wanted to look seductive, they wanted to look like Iris.

Iris Chacón's body personified a Creole sensuality. She established a precedent that put her dancers, the prejudice of society, and macho behavior in the spotlight. When I see old interviews of her and listen to the questions they asked her, and how they looked at her, I see how uncomfortable she was. This was before the Me-too movement. She always managed the disrespect gracefully, and although she seemed to play it off as if it was okay, I am sure she knew it was the price she had to pay to pave the way to a new way of thinking, not only about her work, and herself as a woman, but also the people that worked with her.

Iris Chacón's career emerged at a time when something needed to be shaken in Puerto Rico. I believe she did everything in her power to reach a new level as an artist, and she used every opportunity to try new things. She practiced Buddhism, which was also a new in Puerto Rico, and overall, it was a new time for people to learn about other spiritual, and social practices. She tried to break away from the patriarchal, misogynist, and social norms that insisted on controlling her. In my house, we never missed any of her shows. At first, we saw the show to see her, and later to see my cousin with her. It was a great combo. Walter Mercado and Iris Chacón on the same evening.

In one of her interviews, she expressed how Puerto Rican mothers' body-shamed their daughters for being curvy, and spoke about the social stigma women created on those who dressed a certain way by referring to them as morally loose. Iris wanted to change that narrative, and her work proposed a feminist movement of empowerment, self-love, and a new standard of beauty that changed North American standards. She represented a modern woman who had the power, and the butt to shake her traumas and the opinions of others. She used the vedette persona to be free to do, and say what the other Iris might not have been able to do, because only a shocking image like the one she created could have stopped people in their tracks to "See" what she was doing.

I believe her art represented the emancipation of her body, and the freedom of her dancer's identity. She was a feminist in her right and art. I learned throughout the years how, in crucial times, women will usually be at the forefront of these social, and cultural transformations. Iris Chacón became an art piece as she made art. She also became a sex symbol that slowly educated men about sexuality. She was an advocate for a new community that was rising, and also confronting a tremendous challenge.

Her body was not the slim, chiseled, statuesque figure of Sylvia del Villard, but like Sylvia, her presence was stunning. Both bodies, in their uniqueness, told a story about themselves, about their people, and made history. In an impetuous way, she unlatched a new attitude that impacted female behavior.

There were other sex symbols like Lucy Fabery, La Muñeca de Chocolate, and I must include my aunt, Raquel Caballero. Her artistic name was Sultry. She was a singer, a beautiful woman with a beautiful voice and spectacular body, One of Susana's oldest daughters. She had a bit of a bad mouth, and cursed anyone who crossed the line with her. She also inspired me to be like her. I grew up seeing her dresses, and everything was so shiny, like in the movies. Raquel had a lot of rhinestone earrings and things that I was drawn to. She used to sing in Puerto Rico, and later, she traveled to Mexico, and ended up living in NYC. She would give me some of her stuff to play with, and I remember one day I was looking at her putting some stuff away. In my innocence and ignorance, I asked her when she was going to die so I could keep her stuff. I was a little girl but had heard about how people keep stuff when others die. I remember she laughed and called my mother and said - "Dalin, mira lo que me dijo la hija e' puta de tu hija! Que cuándo me iba a morir para quedarse con mis cosas! Que barbaridad!" I am not sure what my mom said, but Raquel laughed and looked at me. I was a bit scared but then she gave me more things and hugged me. She did not have kids, and I know she loved me as a daughter. When I used to stay with her, she would dance for me and made-up silly songs to make me laugh. Sometimes I would laugh so much until I felt sick to my stomach because she would do these shows for me while I was usually eating dinner or lunch at her house. She was the one who took me to McDonald's for the first time, and as a kid, I thought that was awesome. Her career was short because of many factors, but she had her moments like all of us do, just moments.

These beautiful women, starting with the ones in my family, gifted me with inspirations that I have seen come to fruition. The most important one has been their courage to confront society, claim spaces, set new ways to express who they are, and have a voice. They dared to advocate for others and for what they believed in. These forms of resistance are inevitable forms of evolution that also changed traditional dances like Bomba. Bomba was that safe art, and space where black people were able to be themselves as much as the circumstances allowed it, and because there were always limitations in the physical world, the arts became an escape. In my opinion, the woman who made change happen in the Bomba dance was Mrs. Petra Cepeda Brenes. I do not know of other female Bomba dancers to make any comparisons with, although I have heard that a woman by the name of Ponchinela always comes up as one of the great Bomba dancers of her time, but I did see Petra dancing, and my mother also recalls her as a young woman performing because they went to high school together in Central High School, in Santurce.

Petra Cepeda, in my opinion, took women's Bomba dance to a different level. She also shook her body but differently. She used a prop to shake off the old and bring something new, and that prop was her skirt. Petra was a performer and the choreographer of her family's dance company. She was a multi-talented woman who knew how to engage the audience, and the stage was her home. She added a strong theatrical element to their shows that enhanced every presentation while creating a separate reputation, and style as a performer. Reciting and her gestural language were her forte; it gave her performance a dramatic touch that trapped the audience in her poetry and dance.

Her traditional dance projected a strong, modern woman, and the skirt became her voice. Her dance was unique because although it was traditional, it was not like some elders described women's Bomba dance. There was an expectation that women's dance was supposed to be delicate. Her dance did not only represent a region; it also represented her time, and I will dare say a feminist movement in Bomba. I remember Don Felix Alduen, an elder Bombero from the town of Mayaguez. He once told me that when women danced back in the days of his youth, or at least what he recalled seeing, was women "decorating" men's dance. He said: - "Las mujeres decoraban el baile de los hombres. Eran delicadas y mariposeaban alrededor del bailador con pasos sutiles. Eso que hacen ahora, de mover tanto la falda y de ésa manera violenta, no se veía en aquél entonces. El que pedía al tambor era el caballero." This meant that, according to his experience, women dance used to be subtle, and when they danced, they looked like butterflies, moving around very gently and elegantly around men. There were no abrupt movements of the skirt. Women were not protagonists in Bomba dance, nor had a strong corporeal improvised dance movement. Men were the ones drumming and dancing more expressively in front of the drum. It was something ruled by men, from the music to the dancing. He continued by saying that women hardly moved their skirts; their focus was on their footwork, but it was all very soft and discreet. I found interesting his observations on how he saw women's dance change to a more aggressive style or more expressive one. If he made those observations about women dancing, it was because a significant transformation had happened. I believe that the shift had to do with women's new roles in society, and the need for visibility on and off stage. The region where this happened also informs the dance. Santurce was a place of modernity. Petra's art was influenced by her environment and social experiences as she became a leader in her family's dance company.

I believe Petra Cepeda was responsible for that shift in women's Bomba dance. She presented a new form that seemed to be more dynamic, interactive, and intense. As a tall, slim, black woman, she looked even bigger on stage, and her gestural language made her stand out. She intensified the exchange with the drummer who played the Primo drum. To see her dance was pure drama. This is important because the energy of one person will create a hype, and raise the energy to a level where everyone is giving all they have, and that is when true artistry comes out. That is what artistic collaborations should be about in any performance. The dance became aggressive, as Don Alduen put it. Women in Bomba were being seen, and the way the skirt was manipulated had a lot to do with the image that women were projecting, and how it impacted Bomba music and performance on stage, but mostly women's image. Women's dances with or without props was causing a new style in the performing arts. Petra proposed a new dance style with a skirt, while Sylvia and Iris also did but without one. What Petra proposed in Bomba dance and the others in other dance styles were expressions that exist to this day. Knowingly or not, Petra introduced traditional folk dance into a movement of women's liberation and visibility through improvisation. Petra Cepeda made a statement through her artistry, and her performance represented her creativity. and love for her father's legacy which she shared with others with difficulty. That difficulty or resistance that I refer to is probably because it could not have been easy to share with strangers something that meant so much to her and her family. Doing Bomba was how they clothed and ate. It meant more to them than to any person who claims to be a Bombero (a) (x) today because life was different back then. The same must have happened to Iris Chacón. She shared her body with the world, and that is not easy when people judged and labeled her without understanding the purpose behind her work. These artists and their bodies were a means of evolution for Puerto Rican culture, history, and society.

Petra Cepeda was an innovator and attributed to the Bomba skirt a significance that added character and beauty to Bomba dance. For some, a skirt or layers of clothing can limit movement, while for others, a skirt might add to a dancing vocabulary that enriches the experience. All of the different purposes and results of these changes contributed to the evolution of dance as a form of resistance and a system of self-identity. The 70s and 80s were a time of revolution and resistance by loosening the body and, in Bomba, expanding the skirt.

It was a time for redefining Puerto Rican traditions, and whether it was moving a skirt, shaking hips under skirts that covered their bodies like The Ayala dancers, or shaking her bare hips as Iris did, a change occurred.

Iris Chacón chose to uncover completely to break taboos. Iris and Sylvia dared to make a statement and stand, dance, and be their truth. Ellas hicieron historia con el cuerpo. They did not back down; they knew people were looking and judging and still stood strong and that is enough for me to see how powerful women are and how threatening the female body can be, dressed or not. Now and then, I sing Tú eres caramelo y chocolate while standing on the ball of my feet. I move my body to the beat of memories that reaffirm the beauty and power of being a woman, and I choose to use my skirt when I dance Bomba to celebrate all things that make me, Me, while I honor those who made it easier for me to express myself this way; aggressively, gracefully, and however I believe I need to share what I feel.

Iris Chacón, la Bomba de Puerto Rico, Petra Cepeda, la bailadora de Bomba de Puerto Rico, Sylvia del Villard, la que resistió vestirse de Bomba, and so many others are pillars of this movement that celebrated women's bodies, voices, and political change. I learned from these women the importance of evolving, not competing, because my calling is mine and no one else's. How I chose to dance, and how I move in life is because of the inspiration of the women in my family, and these other divas who have presented themselves to me as muses of vision, movement, courage, and faith. Yo soy caramelo, yo soy chocolate. I am Afro-indigenous mixed with European ancestors. An ancestral heritage that I choose to ignore because it is always in my face like a disrespectful, entitled bitch. I am aware that is there, I need to be to not lose my way.

Yo soy lo que quiero ser, cuando quiero serlo. That is the privilege of mixed ethnicities and cultures. My body and how I move will meet the purpose that is meant for me. Like those before me, I will also shake my body and use my voice, my experience, and temporary truths to make a change because there is nothing absolute except for physical transformation and change.

Thank you, Iris, Sylvia, and Petra, on behalf of many generations of women, and men who owe the freedom of their expressions and identity to your artistry and courage.

Part 7

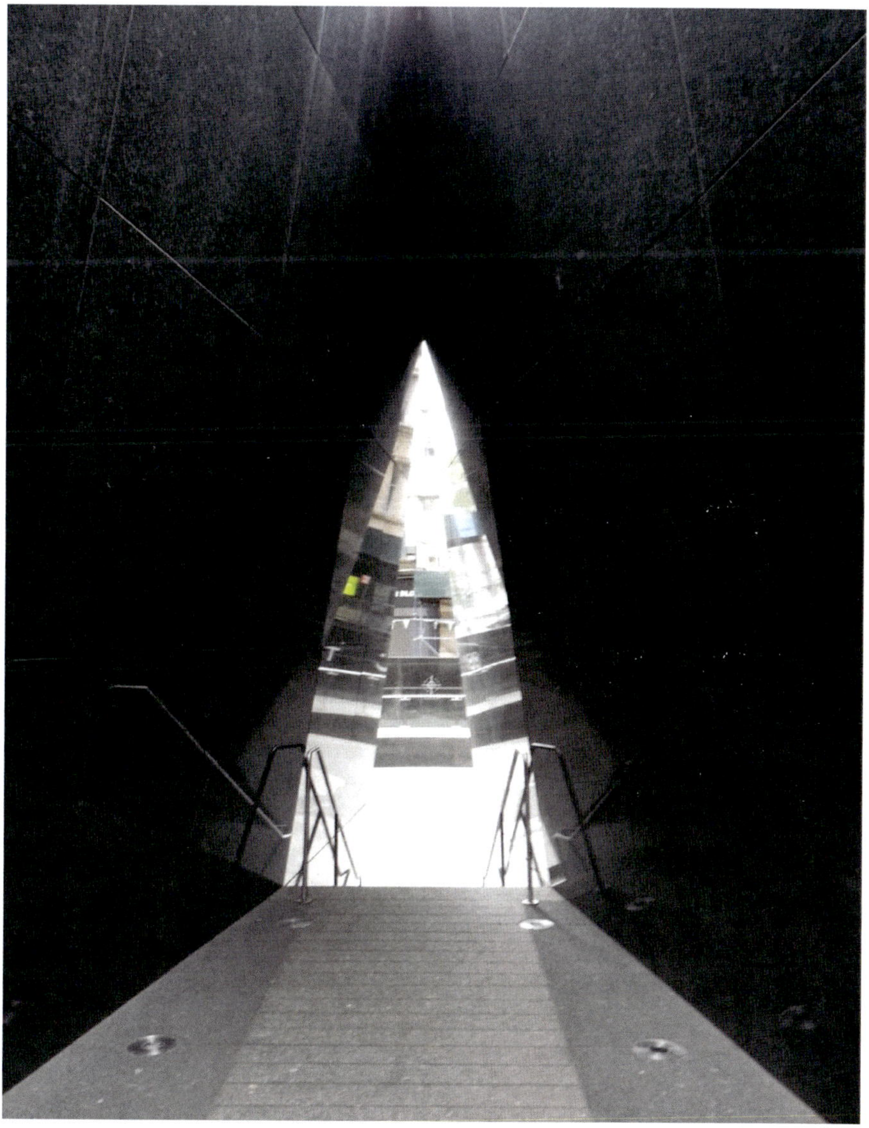

Transformation

Transformations

La vida es tiempo de espera y nos llena de miedo porque sabemos que vamos a morir pero no sabemos cómo, ni cuándo, ni dónde. En esa ansiedad,, reconocemos nuestra brevedad y nos volvemos una mierda porque sabemos que esa transformación a sabe Dios qué, es inevitable. Unos quieren candela, otros quieren que los entierren enteros, y otros ni guardan para ése último evento y no hablan de ello tampoco. La vida es tiempo. Dios es tiempo, y la muerte es también Dios. He visto la venida de Dios en varias ocasiones a recoger a los elegidos, a los que ya han cumplido su tiempo, a los que leyeron de su libro la última página. Lo único que aprecio de esta experiencia que llamo vida y parece un baile con distintos personajes y en distintos escenarios, es que nunca falta el elemento sorpresa. Aún cuando uno sabe que la persona está moribunda frente a uno, la muerte siempre sorprende, como ladrón en la noche o como un regalo sin motivo.

Lucas Figueroa Andino, was a dancer, a very talented person, and my cousin. I adored being with him because he had a wonderful sense of humor, and we loved to dance together. Lucas introduced me to a new identity that I never judged because I loved him, and in doing so, I learned to love others like him. We all struggle with identity issues and the prejudice, biases, and behaviors that come with that. I remember visiting places with him that I never knew existed. I went with him to a gay club for the first time in Puerto Rico. I was a minor, and he was not that much older than me, but he was a Chacón dancer. He made me look older with makeup, or so I thought. Lucas showed me a new world that was prohibited for the straight and the righteous. I had the privilege to see the best drag queen shows, and dance to the best DJs Puerto Rico ever had.

I had the privilege to go to *Bachelor* with him, and know what it was like to be a VIP when I was barely sixteen. Bachelor was a Gay club in Santurce that everyone talked about and wanted to experience, but people were afraid of. Santurce was the place for the avant-garde crowd.

Back then, the night was the time for people of "ambiente" as they used to call it. La vida nocturna was perfect for gay people to come out and meet in these spaces created by them and for them. I loved the dance floor but also enjoyed looking from afar. I would sit in a section that had different levels, and gaze at surreal scenes that not many were able to see at my age. I was never asked to show an ID, and I always went with him; otherwise, that place was not for me in so many ways. I was a minor and straight, but open minded enough to respect and appreciate the creativity that existed in there. Those evenings I spent with Lucas, although they were fun, they used to make me feel sad afterward. Going back to the "norm" was painful, especially for homosexual men and women. Like cimarrones, homosexuals traded the sun for the moon and became free at night. Lucas and I shared both, the Sun and the Moon. During the day he was pretty much the same unless his father was around.

Our lives changed as we grew older, and we also changed although we did not grow apart. We just had different paths to follow. Lucas went his way, and I went mine, but for both of us, it was a time for radical changes and sacrifices.

Lucas kept doing his thing in his world, dancing with Iris Chacón, and I was doing other stuff that were not as glamorous, but they brought me joy. Time accelerated, and with that same speed, Aids appeared, chaos broke loose, and fear took over the world. Suddenly, everything changed again, but this time, it brought upon the gay community the blame and responsibility for the health of the nation and, dare I say, the world. Every magazine, newspaper, news, and gossip covered the topic that made people uneasy. I can compare it with how COVID-19 made us feel and how information or misinformation had an impactful effect on how we lived and shared with our own families. The paranoia, fear, and separation of people in Puerto Rico were intense. People's reaction to Aids was even worse in New York City. People began to panic and behave differently, and homophobia got stronger than ever.

Many artists contracted the disease, and among them were some of Iris Chacón's dancers. There were constant talks about testing for the virus, how people got infected, the exaggerations of it all, and people had a lot of anxiety. I also feared for my cousin and wanted to see him to know what he was doing in the midst of that nightmare. I visited him at his mom's, and that day, I sensed something was off. We talked and laughed as usual. He told me about what he was doing, but I knew he was not himself. Later that day, he told me he was sick. My body froze. The news seemed unreal. Immediately, I sort of blocked the information from my mind and shut my emotions, but there was a roller coaster of feelings in me. There he was, physically looking better than ever, but his eyes were full of fear. I noticed how he spoke, and my cousin, my loving friend, was desperate. His friends were dying, and I guess he knew his luck was not going to be different than theirs. He had always been slim and fit, and ironically, he had gained weight and looked so strong and healthy. He coped with the situation as the great artist that he was. I coped with it the best that I could, going along as his dance partner that I was. I did not ask; I did not force any type of conversation that would break him. He led, and I followed; he pretended, and so did I, and without saying anything, we both shared a different conversation with our eyes, holding hands and laughing about stuff as if nothing was happening. He was not dancing as before but tried to keep busy to ignore his illness. He was not in denial but was not ready to speak openly about it with anyone.

We talked about his plans and my life. He kept his humor, but this weird energy surrounded him, and we both felt time was running out. Death witnessed our conversations, and we both knew it. Tension hid behind smiles that distracted us from the truth. His mother was devastated even though she kept her calm. When I think of her, I think about the strength that God must have given her to deal with such pain and how she learned to let go even before he died. His transition was quick. He was home when the fevers started and made him delirious, and his brother was there to help him, but we were all dealing with something nobody understood or knew what to do. It was like watching a shooting star leave us. Everything happened very fast, which, in a way, was good for him and for all of us who loved him and did not want to see him deteriorate and suffer a long and inevitable death. I think about transitions and how we feel about them. Even when dancing, to transition in a choreography, we need to release a certain amount of energy and focus and, most importantly, have the willingness to change with poise, whether it might be to do a different step or leave the stage and let others take your place.

One afternoon, I went to visit his mom. She gave me the news that he had been in the hospital for a couple of days because he had pneumonia. I did not have the strength to get upset over the fact that I was not informed sooner.

We were having a conversation about him when the phone rang. I drove her to Centro Médico in Rio Piedras because they wanted her to see him. He was in critical condition. When we entered the room, he was lying with his eyes closed. His lungs were filled with so much water that when he breathed, it sounded as if he was gargling. She stood beside him, and I stood at the end of the bed and held his feet, which were uncovered. They were cold, and the skin felt different. It was a coldness that I had not felt before. The cold came from inside his body. He was dying in front of us, and then and there, he taught me that death enters the body through the feet. I put on a pair of socks and rubbed his feet while she prayed silently and spoke to him softly. She said her goodbyes, and I knew she told his spirit to leave in peace. I prayed with her, and even though we knew what was going to happen, I wanted to comfort her. She knew that he was going to transition before she received that call, and that I am sure of.

I held her hand, and at the same time, my mind went blank. Sometimes silence is good, and the best thing to do is be there and let the spirit do the talking. What can anyone say to a mother who is about to lose her child? He was her star, her joy, and she only knew what she had to put up with and the dreams and secret conversations she cherished and kept because it was her child. How can you comfort a mother who is looking at her son and perhaps is not seeing the man before her but the boy she gave birth to, raised, loved, and accepted for who he was, understanding that God does not make mistakes.

I looked at his physical body, appreciating him and God for the opportunity of sharing with such an extraordinary human being. He taught me acceptance and tolerance, not by ignoring, but by seeing the person, seeing who they are, and loving unconditionally. Even though he had his eyes shut and could not speak, I know he heard us in the middle of the struggle of letting go of his material body. We stood with him until the nurse asked us to leave. As we walked through the hallways, I cannot express how I felt. Still, while I write, I cannot define that feeling. Detachment is a great teacher but is a bitch nonetheless.

On the drive back to her house, she was quiet and smoked a cigarette. There we were, the both of us, witnesses of how powerful death is. Grateful for how delicate and considerate death can be. By allowing a mother to say her goodbyes to the son that I know brightened her days and made us laugh, and we both loved. I was humbled for allowing me to share that last time with my friend, my blood, and my dance partner. When I dropped her off, I asked her if she wanted me to stay with her. She replied no, and I understood she needed her time. I asked her to call me if she needed anything, and between the time I left her and I got home, she got the call that he passed away. I am not sure how I recovered from his loss. I think of him as if he is still alive and we just live apart. He stepped out of the closet, danced with Iris, lived his dream, lived his life how he wanted, and perhaps he was a shooting star that was meant to be here for a brief moment, like all of us, because time is irrelevant and we should focus on enjoying the moment. For him, subió y bajó su telón and physically, that was that, but he left a lot in my heart that still lives on.

During the time he was with me, he was bright, and his mind and soul gave me so many happy moments and laughs that I cannot remember him with sadness. I loved him and everything he was and wanted to be. I knew it was not easy, but he was determined to shine, and so he did, and that is inspirational. Many years later, after that moment in my life, a dear friend of mine also created a transition for himself that transformed Bomba.

He dared to come out to dance using a skirt in a Bomba dance, and then and there, magically, he broke a societal curse that allowed men who identified as they pleased to dance Bomba with a skirt to this day. He freed the skirt from gender limitations, and as wings, others were able to express themselves more creatively.

Lionel Villahermosa also paid a price for breaking tradition. His actions put in the spot many of his so-called friends who judged and criticized him for daring to be himself. His process was harsh, and that evening, when it happened, it even inspired someone to write a song about Un Gay. I am not sure how many people apologized to him or stood firm in their belief, which is fine too, but if we are more than just our bodies and if, in this case, Bomba is supposed to be used to build, we should rethink how we create spaces. We should think about how traditions create identities, egos that no longer serve us, and how the roles we play can create better and more tolerant communities for art to thrive. We should also think of how as some become free to express themselves, women still need to struggle to do the same, to have rights, to be seen and heard, to have safe spaces that at some points are shared with others, and that suddenly the script changes and the good deed is punished. As we transform things it is important to not sell ourselves short. As things change, we need to guarantee that things are equal, and that the blessings and evolutions of some, does not happen at the expense of others. Let us evolve in a healthy way where we can all get to whatever side we need to be, whole, joyful, dignified, truthful, and in peace.

Part 8

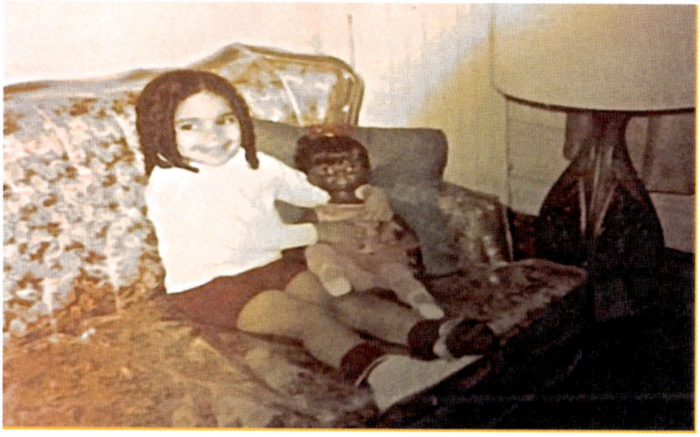

1970s
My ballerina doll and I.

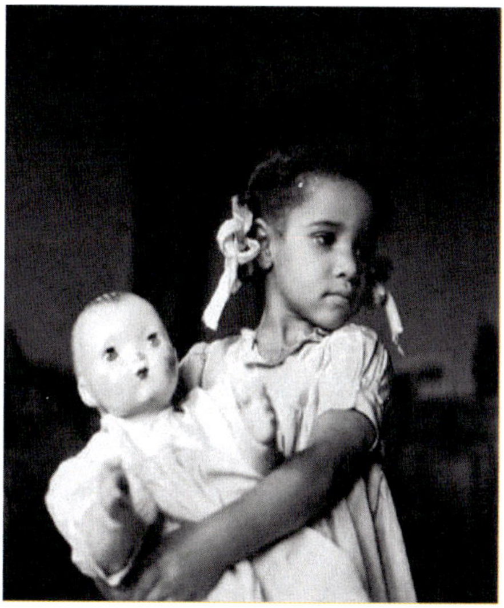

1940s research found Black girls preferred white dolls, and ascribed the preference to the girls' feelings of inferior status.
Charles Hewitt/ Getty Images

Me, Myself, and We

Magic mirror on the wall, who am I?

Migration starts with the imagination. People migrate for various reasons, but the courage to move comes from an idea of better places and better lives. The idea that there is a place where grasses grow greener. People hope they will do better somewhere else and until they get to that destination, that believe keeps them trying to get there. Migration is a difficult process of adjustment and assimilation that makes people change. Puerto Ricans face the same challenges as any other immigrant group without the assistance they need or the opportunity for a fresh start because of our political conditions. We have the so-called privilege of an American citizenship that makes it hard to change our fate. My parents migrated, faced the challenges, and made it to NY and back to Puerto Rico. They knew what they wanted and paid attention to the cue to leave. I on the other hand had a different experience. A bitter sweet relationship with a city that some call it La Universidad de la Vida. A city that I love with all its flaws. A city that gifts me with diversity, intensity, dark humor, and all sorts of energy.

Being a Nuyorican, according to people on the island, made me different. I did not feel different, but in comparison with Puerto Ricans that lived in Puerto Rico, I knew I was. I really did not understand what that difference meant, but it was more about the way they made me feel. I was already used to the idea of being different, because that is very common in NYC. My parents told me that what was important was to never forget that nobody is better than me, and I was not better than anyone else, we all had dignidad. As a kid I spent a lot of time in front of mirrors, metaphorically speaking. "I" became interesting to me. The concept of self and that reflection of a "Yo" was never absolute. These experiences did not necessarily happen in front of a mirror either. I saw myself in the eyes and opinions of others, in their behavior towards me, whether it was good or bad I was constantly learning about myself. I was compared, analyzed, observed, and either accepted or rejected but always seen. I learned that no matter if I was in NYC or Puerto Rico, some of the judgments and behaviors

I dealt with had to do with who was looking at me, and their belief of a made up ideal of a national authenticity or the color of the skin.

In the process of understanding differences, I learned to find similarities, and those mirrors suddenly became important. I started finding the resemblance of others in me. I learned to observe because whenever I felt comfortable, or when I felt I did not fit in, the safest thing to do was to watch people and what they did.

I don't remember paying attention to what I looked like when I was a kid until I went to school. What I remember is a feeling of nostalgia because of the people, places, and the things I missed depending on where I was. When I was in New York during the winter, I thought of sunny afternoons and warm breezes that carried smells of tropical fruits and gardenias, which was my mother's favorite flower. I imagined bright green plátano leaves covering me and my cousins in a patio. The warmth of the island and eating limber while we laughed, and felt protected and loved. Recordar es vivir and kids do it too! Those memories of blue skies and big warm houses with many rooms, and open spaces gave me happiness. Those memories made me want to do things differently.

In school, I drew differently from the other kids. My colors were more intense, and my suns were a brighter yellow, and shined on everything else in my picture. I colored myself darker and drew flowers that my teachers had never seen before. They didn't know about different palm trees, or that coconut water was sweet and delicious, or the different candies that you can make with it. They had never seen the beautiful water of the beaches where I bathed in, where the water could be warm, and so clear that you could see your feet. They never understood the songs I sang or tasted the food I ate at lunch break. On the other hand, they knew things I didn't. I didn't understand why some girls didn't want to play me or others that looked like me, while the ones that looked like me pulled me away from them because they knew. They undid my ponytails to braid my hair, which always got me in trouble when I got home. They taught me games where I had to move my body, and sing at the same time, like a choreography that sped up each time. They also taught me that I shouldn't befriend white girls. Meanwhile, in the classroom I shared a desk with a white boy that could not be sweeter to me. I admit that there were many things I did not understand.

I was in third grade when things started to sink in. In school I was Puerto Rican and I was black, but not black enough. I was a girl but different from the others. I was bilingual, which gave me the advantage of cursing in a language that other kids did not understand, and my parents didn't know I was fluent in. I was in a catholic school and had to deal with the fear of the Lord's anger, and the bad humor of nuns who only knew how to take the fun out of learning.

When I was home, I would forget about the labels I had to wear in school and how much I hated it. The only place I felt understood was at home with my family. As soon as I entered the courtyard of the building where we used to live, I could hear La Fania, and smell sofrito mixed with curry on my way upstairs. In New York City I had a Rican home. It was a small apartment compared to our house in Puerto Rico, but big enough for us. An intimate space inside a bigger box. Like a Russian doll, this big box had many little boxes inside decorated with squares and rectangles everywhere. I remember looking at the building from the outside and focusing on each of those little shapes that told different stories. Sometimes, I locked eyes for brief seconds with neighbors looking out their windows with sad faces blowing smoke out their mouths and nostrils. If I listened hard enough, I could hear people from different places of the world speaking in different languages, some like mine and others that sounded like consonants put together without vowels. I witnessed people's struggles and moments of nothingness. There were times that some stories ended with blue cars with red lights dancing in circles that took the characters away.

Some of our family members lived in the same building as we did. I only had two friends there. One was African American and the other was Pakistani. That place became a little cabildo for us in The Bronx. When I visited my friend Annie's apartment, curry smells left without permission hidden in my clothes, and my mom immediately knew I had gone to her house. In Jackie's apartment, I never really noticed any particular smells, but her mom always gave me half of a red ruby grapefruit sprinkled with sugar. She had a black Great Dane that scratched me once. They were very quiet people, and it felt as if it was always seven o'clock in her house, always dark with a dim light, and the dog was part of the decor. The kitchen was quiet, unlike Puerto Rican kitchens, where visitors like to talk while they cook and sometimes do not even pass the cocina to go to the living room.

Our apartment was always bright. My mother always had the shades or curtains up. She hated dark apartments. Only during winter nights my mother put the curtains down. Other people's cultures, their foods, how they spoke, smelled, sounded, how they danced, walked, talked, and played became an important part of my life. I did not get tired of observing, and wondering how it must have felt like to live in their bodies or wondering what their apartments looked like. Perhaps that was a weird thing to do, but the consciousness of self in such a diverse and complicated space is something that kids often deal with. New York City molded my perception of life and myself in it. I, too, was creating a collage of gestures and movements that I watched from my family and the people around me. In that process of becoming someone, I guess I wanted to be like some of them without realizing that I was already an extension of them in many ways, and a reflection of others too.

Both my parents were set in their cultural ways, and my mother was very militant when it came to her Puerto Rican traditions that were passed on to her. She knew them well because she migrated when she was 18 years old. My father was more open and eclectic. He, too was very puertorriqueño, but he enjoyed the multicultural life.

Media was also an important part of my upbringing. I used to watch Sesame Street and Electric Company. I listened to Roberta Flag, Dionne Warwick, John Coltrane, and Miles Davis because my father loved music. I danced to Tito Rodriguez and La Fania All-Star with my aunt Olga. I loved Soul Train dancers, who showed me the latest dance moves that I practiced at home and with my friends. I sang Miriam Makeba's song Pata Pata and Willie Bobo's Fried Neckbones and some home fries. My aunt called me Popa en Nueva York because I had a purse where I would save the money my father gave me. My father loved Jazz, art, and money, and his spiritual beliefs were a mix of espiritus chinos and africanos. He dressed impeccably. He used to take me to Aqueduct Race Track to see the horses, and pass by

Chinatown afterward to eat and buy me toys. I admired him, loved him, and valued all the things he taught me to this day.

I appreciated the savory mix of Latin sounds and English words that blended into my tradition. My favorite group was The Jackson Five. Michael was my boyfriend. Actually, I had a few, like Muhammed Ali and Bruce Lee.

Television and the Movie Theater reshaped and informed people the same way they do now. Migration increased and Boricuas were moving to NYC by the dozens. Back then, The Bronx and Harlem smelled like a world's market where different spices, languages, and music met. I also spent a lot of time with my aunt, and my cousins in Astoria. That was another home for me. Olga, my mother-aunt, was that cool Titi who was modern, open-minded; and a smart, beautiful woman whom I loved dearly and miss so much. She also raised me and loved me in ways that left no doubt of how she felt for me. She was more than just my aunt. She, too, sang like my grandmother and danced beautifully. I loved going to her house because she always had a party to go to, and of course, I was usually her plus one.

I remember that I disliked wearing pants, so when I stayed at Olga's house, I was one of the cowboys, and carried my plastic gun everywhere but wearing my dresses. I was raised with boys and I was always one of the superheroes they thought I could be to complete their game. I was the youngest, so they would toss me from one bed to the other with a cape made of a towel. I was always hoping not to hurt myself, because I knew it would be worst if my aunt found out, but we would keep playing and thugging it out. At my mom's, I played with dolls in a separate apartment I had made for myself, as I mentioned before. Whenever I went to Puerto Rico, I never played indoors. Me and my cousins never did. The whole idea was to be outside enjoying the weather, and wearing the least amount of clothes as possible to enjoy the sun.

The '70s was a powerful time. I remember seeing news and hearing conversations about Women, Media, African-American people, Puerto Ricans, and Social Justice. There was a constant association between crime, negative stereotypes, and our people.

As a child, I learned about racism because I lived it in my own way, and also saw how black became beautiful on TV. There were two separate narratives going on. It was an era of liberation, and although not everyone was fighting for the same freedom, society was changing. TV shows empowered my blackness, mostly from an African-American perspective, as I also learned how my family defined theirs. My family had a different way of feeling about their blackness as Afro-Puerto Ricans. Skin color was not an issue for them because they knew they were black, and felt there was no need to justify or explain who they were. They, too, were learning about African American culture, the system, and all the other cultures of the people they worked with while living their truth as Puerto Ricans. I am proud to say that they never changed, they loved their traditions and identity. They taught me well to make sure I held on tight to their teachings. They did not change their language, beliefs, including their values.

While I was growing up, I was also trying to understand the minds of Puerto Rican people from the island, and those who created a hybrid culture with what they had in NY. Those who created their ideas of what a Puerto Rican and Puerto Rico were, relied mostly on the memories of others and a need of belonging. Interestingly enough, in most cases they had never visited Puerto Rico. These ideas of patriotism and how to be a Boricua were passed down by their grandparents. Everything around me seemed to be focused on people's identity and the quality of life the system had set for them. That made me aware of what I really liked, which was art, the art made by black people. I grew up watching African-American artists, that we called morenos, on national TV. I also saw Puerto Ricans like Rita Moreno, José Feliciano, María Figueroa from Sesame Street to mention a few, and it felt good; it was like watching family members on TV. But what I remember the most about Puerto Ricans and also Cubans who I thought were Puerto Ricans, were their accent and their voices. The voices of great artists lived in our homes trapped in vinyl records that were played over and over.

African Americans and Caribbeans were connected in many ways and through music and dance our relationship grew stronger. We shared the same roots, we were all victims of racism, but we also shared an inner beat in our spirits that brought us together as a people. Those connections and the circumstances we faced made us creative and resilient. Hip Hop is proof of that power, amongst other social and political movements of the time.

Representation becomes a daily exercise for people in multicultural cities. I had to represent my family, and where I came from even if I wasn't born there. I had to represent my beliefs, and to learn how to negotiate these things as I interacted with others while also being a child. I think that crossing a cultural bridge between Puerto Rico and New York City made me develop what I call a chameleon effect. When in Puerto Rico, I did as Puerto Ricans did, although I was Nuyorican to them, and when in New York City, I did as New Yorkers did, although for them, I was a Puerto Rican. This process of integration, assimilation, and identification can be confusing for a kid. I think there were times I disidentified with everything around me. There were times I did not want to fit in because it was never enough. Like I said before, I was not white enough, not black enough, not Puerto Rican enough, and not American enough. The upside is that you learn to be yourself and lead. I did not feel a necessity to follow or be a part of something, unless it was something that made me feel something special. It was not about exterior stuff; it was about how I felt. I learned to be okay with the idea of being different, whatever that meant, and doing what I needed to do without focusing on what my body meant for others. It takes a while to understand how important and resourceful we are. It is not until you are older, that you understand the game the system has created for us.

When I think of all the things children go through in schools in the United States and Puerto Rico, it frustrates me because I know how the system divest black and brown children from the things that gives them a sense of self and dignity. The deconstruction of identity conditions people to live in a confused state where they don't know how powerful they are and that their power is hidden in their culture; their roots. White people know that, and that is why they have been busy on the cultural appropriation business. They appropriate others cultures, and after they deform it, they sell it back to whoever they stole it from as a product created by them. They do these things without any remorse because for most of them other people's lives are just business as usual. I know that all white people are not bad or racist, but the same way they generalize when it comes to us, it is hard for me not to practice what they taught me. The truth is that the fruit does not fall too far from the tree, and everyone in this novela is conditioned to play these social antagonist roles where the only protagonist is the dollar. Children in the United States grow up looking at tampered mirrors where most of them end up construing an identity from a place of insecurity, shame, and a sense of unworthiness.

My experience with other Puerto Rican kids was also interesting. I identified more with African Americans than with Puerto Ricans because a lot of Puerto Rican immigrants of my generation were from el campo. I was a city girl in New York and in Puerto Rico. The kids I knew and I had different experiences in Puerto Rico. We even spoke differently.

My family never took me to the campo when we visited the island. They shared with family, and took care of their stuff, so maybe there was not enough time. It was in NYC that I eventually met people from the countryside. It was also then that I learned that they too were racist. On the other hand, I would hear some Puerto Ricans from the coast calling them jíbaros, and saying they were not to be trusted because they were unos agusao', which means sneaky. There were different Boricua boxes that identified us, and the color of the skin seemed to be important in this mess too. I grew up trying to break boxes and unfortunately putting others in one, because that is what the system teaches you. I looked in mirrors imagining who I would be in the future, and seeing the future in my reflection.

Bomba also became a mirror for me. I found a new way to show my identity through this artistry. To me, la Bomba es negra. It can belong to everybody but it is first black, then Puerto Rican, and after those two it can be whatever and for whomever. The proliferation of Bomba has served as a mirror to question Puerto Rican identity and forces us to take a closer look at the complexities of our social constructions. It has also presented an issue of representation on stage due to our history of mestizaje that creates a contradiction between what we say, what we look like, and what people might understand. I believe that because now there is an awareness of appropriation, we should educate the spectators, even if it is briefly, about our history and why we look the way we do, and claim this art even though there might not be any dark skinned, black bodies participating in these groups.

It is time to fix what has been damaged for the sake of our children, and do things with the consciousness that we are all colonized, and these traditions that we preserve need to be evaluated. It is time to admit that there is racism in Puerto Rico. I see the intentions and people talking about it. They use all these interesting wording but that does not fix the problem. I still have not seen an antiracist plan in action taking place with consistency, especially in elementary schools where is needed the most. That idea of being someone, el Yo soy, and the process of learning how to be someone, starts at an early age, with objects, words, and most importantly adults' behaviors towards topics that need to be discussed. The feelings attached to the things, sounds, and people around them will always affect them and how they see themselves in this world.

This is why art plays a significant role in the discourse of national and individual identity. Art becomes a mirror that starts conversations about topics that otherwise might be difficult to have. The process of identity is never-ending, and as time goes by, we learn more about who we are in the spaces we choose to be. At some point in my life, I chose to be on stage and on that platform the information from my childhood, and whatever I learned, and unlearned after that was revealed in the ways I could express it. I became a mirror for others the moment I chose art. I became a political and educational resource that without big speeches, I began re-educating the spectators as I also learned from them.

I was and continue to be part of a movement that changed the scripted narratives that were designed in the 60s that whitewashed Puerto Rican black culture. That proposal transformed Bomba into Puerto Rican folklore, and slowly removed the black body as the main representative of this expression and renamed it without making the black part too obvious. It became Bomba puertorriqueña. It was in New York City that it became Afro-Puerto Rican. The experience of interacting with black people from all over the world changes our definitions of blackness. The experience of sharing cultures, information, and spaces re-teaches us about our history as Caribbeans, and as black people.

I will finish with a recuerdo about a doll. The day I chose my first black doll. I went with my mother to a store in The Bronx. A new doll came out; she was a ballerina, and I had seen it on TV. They had them white with blonde hair and black ones with jet-black hair. We were standing in front of the dolls, and immediately I was drawn to the black doll, but I remember hesitating. My mother noticed I looked at the black one first and then saw my indecision. It was then that she stepped in and told me how beautiful the black doll was and encouraged me to get her. She told me that if that was the one that I liked, because my face lit up, I should get it. I left the store happy with, and also with a weird feeling that I did not understand.

My mother taught me a beautiful lesson that day, not necessarily about racism or decision-making, but about how she viewed herself and her people. My mother used that moment to reassure me that black is beautiful, and that although my skin color was not as dark as the doll's, I was being represented. When I went back home to share with my friends, Jackie, the African-American one, looked at the doll without any emotion and did not even ask me to touch or play with the doll. I did not understand, but I felt the confirmation of the reason why I hesitated without being able to explain it in depth. I just remember being sad for my doll because of not knowing how my friends would react, I guess. That object meant something important to me. I played with my doll at home, she and I alone, and when I played with my friends, we used her white dolls. I did not want my doll to be rejected because I knew I would have to stop playing with my friends. I chose to avoid breaking up our friendship, but I never felt the same way playing with her again. My doll was beautiful like my mom, like my grandmother, like all the girls, and women in my family. I believed my doll was beautiful like Jackie, although she did not see it. Time passed by, she moved, and so did I. Since then, many mirrors kept showing up in my life, and when I had my son, I wanted to be one for him. I wanted to be that mirror, that when he looked at me and saw himself as a part of me, he could see how important, valuable, and beautiful human being he is, and how loved and special he is. He gifted me with a grandson and part of my mission is to teach my grandson that no one needs to tell him who he is or define his potential for him. I want him to learn that whenever he stands in front of any mirror is to reaffirm his presence on this earth, by being his authentic self, and if he needs to break a few mirrors, boxes, and friendships in his journey, that will be fine too and we will be standing by his side to support and encourage him

Part 9

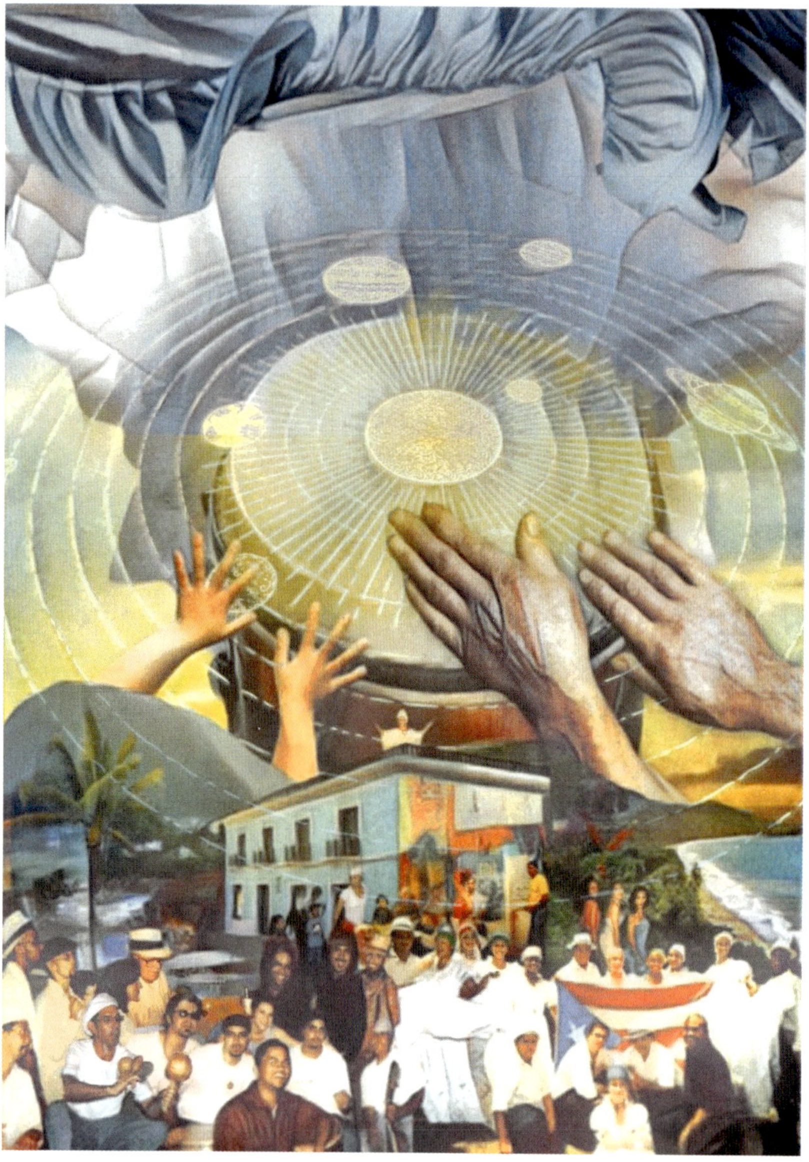

Revestida

The image of a Neo Bomba

I dance in a circle. I dance with stories, people, and memories. In the center, a sense of I, of we, of everything and nothing. This dichotomy of my attachment to tradition but the need for change, guarantees permanence within change and freedom within a structure for identity's sake. In that circle, I find myself with others, and together, we make history, build new narratives about the future, and we also create memories as we become elders. In those circles, I'm sometimes a witness, others a protagonist, looking from afar, waiting for the moment or the right feeling that tells me when it's okay to stroll in it and continue a pattern to preserve a habit or be disruptive and break them to start something new. I've danced in many circles that sometimes feel like bliss and can also feel asphyxiating, like being stuck, like a slow death that warns me when it's time to move and expand. I avoid being trapped by insularism and monotony. My spirit always whispers to my body when it is time to re-imagine, renovate, and go on new adventures.

Time is where ideas and dimensions cross and where the past is always present. Bomba remerged in Puerto Rico at different times, but in the 90s Bomba came back in a very unique way. A movement began, ignited by a desire to change stuff around, and what we did has lasted to this day. We, a relatively small group of people wanted to do Bomba and that had many meanings. We changed the traditional, folkloric Bomba into a Neo Folk Bomba. A contemporary art that represented the past and was always time traveling. Bomba became addictive. As any drug, Bomba was negotiated, demanded, and it grew. It was about supply and demand, and also about the creative ways to sell it. Bomba became trendy, fabulosa, y se plantó con fuerza. Like a seed, Bomba had been planted in us by our elders, and perhaps the fruits were not what they expected, but it surely exceeded the expectations, although not in the ways that most elders would have wanted.

After Don Rafael Cepeda Atiles's passing in 1996, a group of people started reshaping the standards of how Bomba was going to be done. It was a challenging mission of mixing the old with the new, and respecting the legacy that was given to us. This phenomenon called Bomba was in the hands of people who were willing to give her a makeover and put in the work. I was part of that group of Bomberos who believed in changing the game and felt somewhat ready to move forward. We just needed our mentors to trust us, and trust that what they taught us would be enough to continue their work. I personally had a good relationship with my teachers and Bomba elders. I invested time with them listening to their stories, and learning everything I know from them. We also shared other moments that were about family.

In the making of a Neo Bomba, some values changed, and also relationships, but change is always uncomfortable and at the beginning can be a bit rocky. But even with all the difficulties, everyone involved in this movement had a good foundation to move forward and revolutionize Puerto Rico with the beat of Bomba drums.

Most of us had experience performing with Bomba renowned families and knew how to adjust to whatever the need was. We were good on stage and doing Bomba off stage. We knew how to teach and overall represent Bomba in a way that became relevant to younger people. We possessed the skills and knowledge to change things responsibly. We also knew what to change and what should not because the essence of what Bomba is relies on its foundation.

As I had mentioned before, I see Bomba as a woman with a strong identity who knows what she needs to survive, and that is her mission; survival. I believe Bomba has a mind of its own and choses people. The movement was not meant to dismiss the attires, props, or songs that told her story, but rather to create new ones because everything evolves, and so did she. That old image no longer served her because a lot of young people were not into watching folkloric dance companies. They did not pay attention because with evolution the culture transforms and because of Puerto Rico's status, our culture is always being influenced by others.

Like Bomba, I was changing, maturing, and slowly creating my Paseo, which means a stroll. Paseo is the basic part of the dance, and something that every Bomba dancer does, or should do, before beginning to improvise. This stroll was leading me to an adventure that has lasted to this moment that I write about it. Needless to say, Bomba was also changing us in this makeover process. Both our image was changing, and our roles were shifting to break the norm. Back then, Bomba became my medicine. It was time to set Bomba off and revestirla con pinta de progresista and make her desirable.

In this new mission I became a different woman, a different mother, and a different facilitator with a renewed sense of how I wanted to live, to guide others, how to do my art, and who I wanted to be in the Bomba world, which was complicated because I was in Puerto Rico, but my mind was still of a Nuyorican. I had to learn things and unlearn others to flow with these needs and changes of that particular time. Bomba became more relaxed with a modern sound that rippled its way to the ears of new audiences. Bomba even moved from stages to nontraditional spaces that became cultural niches and attracted a lot of people who had never heard or seen Bomba before.

I must make a parenthesis to thank all the people who opened their homes to give Bomba one, and to all the people who created museums, bars, empty spaces in a park, centers, and so many other places into learning spaces where we practiced and kept our elder's stories, made new friends, and built communities.

I believe this modern Bomba exploded between 1997 and 1998. It was a time for the birth of Urban Bomba. The área metro became the center of a socio-cultural, and economic movement for the arts in general, but also for Bomba. The Cepeda family had already created the concept of an urban Bomba while wearing the folkloric clothing. They had their style and the Bomba of Santurce became a trend and it also impacted Bomba in other regions of Puerto Rico, especially the Bomba of Loiza. Our style, the Cepeda's styl,e or Santurce style, defined us as dancers and drummers. The reason why I mention Loiza, is because the way they do Bomba is very different than other regions in Puerto Rico. This happened because at the time, many Santurce teaching artists began teaching in Piñones, and their dance changed Loiza's style, specifically for women. A fusion began happening due to this interaction. The reason for this shift was not only about Bomba.

Leaders were concerned about the violence in their communities and were looking for ways to engage Youth in something cultural, dynamic, and also taught by young people to make it more appealing.

Lately, I have observed how Bomba's variegated styles have slowly merged into one. Now, the challenge is to find people who know how to drum and dance Bomba in the style of their particular regions, and with all the characteristics that distinguished Bomba from the west coast to Bomba from the south, and north of Puerto Rico.
In the late 90s, Bomba was still portrayed on stage with pompous costumes that inspired some, and others did not like it, but most importantly, Bomba was becoming something everyone wanted to learn because of what was happening off stage. We were not a big group, but we made so much noise that everyone heard about us. As we became the new folklorists and faces of Bomba. Its image was changing nationally and transnationally. It was a contrapunto that disrupted tradition in many ways.

The purpose of this movement was to make new memories, tell new stories, sing new songs, document these transformations in new formats, and create and use Bomba as a tool that served other kinds of music, other dances, other genres, and ways of expression. We were moving forward but without forgetting our roots, the foundation, and the respect that our elders deserved. At least on my part, I always shared my ideas and projects with those who taught me. They supported me and I was able to build an artistic identity that began as with my elder's blessing as a dancer, and later as artistic director and producer, to this day.

We detached Bomba from unreachable stages, and we also detached Bomba from Plena, which, at the time, due to people's ignorance, they always mentioned Bomba and Plena together as if they were the same thing. We created spaces called "Talleres de Bomba," which were exclusively for learning how to dance and drum this genre. Even the concept of performing Bomba changed. We made plazas, pubs, schools, parks, and everywhere where people had access to, a stage that included spectators in our performances. Like a machete, this movement cut the boundaries that prevented people from feeling, hearing, and moving to Bomba rhythms. I too, created my teaching spaces surrounded by other forms of art that inspired my work because I did most of my workshops in different museums in Old San Juan. I was surrounded by visual art and historical places that inspired me as I collaborated with facilitators who sponsored my initiatives. Mr. Jorge Negron opened a space for artists to share their knowledge on the art of making drums, playing them, dancing Bomba, and everything related to an African legacy that was slowly fading and was about to disappear if nothing was done about it. The Museum of the African Root, in Old San Juan was one of those places that became super important for Puerto Rican black culture, and because of Mr. Negron's vision, he made the space accessible for every proposal that served as a cultural and artistic platform. The irony of it all is that this place where all the "negrura" was taking place was next to Pablo Casals' Museum. Mr. Casal was a cellist known for his classical compositions and plenty of times my workshops were at capacity and they had to lend us their space to fit more people.

All of those opportunities made Bomba visible to an audience that had been waiting for a new interpretation of one of Puerto Rican cultural expressions. People needed a new form of identity. Bomba was the driving force guiding us, breaking every rule and transforming spaces into Bomba spots where followers fell under her spell. Old San Juan became my workspace, home base, stage, and chill-out spot. I would drive up Norzagaray Street to teach at the Museo de la Raíz Africana, Galería Nacional, and Casablanca Museum. I also performed in any of the plazas, hotels, and businesses in the capital. Once again, an urban setting set the tone for a special kind of Bomba that was performed in various streets, bars, plazas, museums, and even in a Nuyorican Cafe in Puerto Rico that also helped to put her in a spot, and for tourists to visit after Rumba was closed. Rumba was a bar that became a church for many, and was one of the first places where this Neo Bomba first appeared. Sundays became the day for some to go to church, and others made Bomba and Rumba their sacred place.

One of the initiatives that also helped Bomba was the Banco Popular's annual Christmas special. Banco Popular de Puerto Rico had started doing Christmas specials with Puerto Rican artists that were televised, and these specials were also sold in DVD formats. In

2004, Paloma Suau, the daughter of Gabriel Suau, a Spaniard who had moved to Puerto Rico and was also changing TV shows and the concept of censorship, was interested in doing something focused on Plena and Bomba. Paloma Suau was the director of this particular Christmas special they called RAICES.

Her staff went on a mission to find Bomba and Plena performers. They found musical groups, researched Bomba and Plena's history, and created a balance that made the final work educational while keeping the usual renowned artists that people loved and artistic performances, but this time, they included Bomba dancers and drummers. They held auditions to choose the Bomba dancers and groups that would participate, but at the time, I didn't know anything about it, and nobody had told me about it either. I worked as a school teacher, and my time was very compromised. It wasn't until later that I found out that most of the people that I worked with knew already, but for whatever reason, everyone was keeping the information as if it were a secret. While people were going to auditions or had their appointments to attend one, I went one evening to Rumba where Son del Batey, a Bomba group directed by Omar "Pipo" Sánchez, used to perform. That evening I danced as usual. It was an informal thing that everyone who felt like dancing could join them on stage. I remember wanting to dance to one of my favorite Bomba songs, and when I finished, as I was coming down the steps, a hand reached out and grabbed me. When I looked, it was a young woman with blonde hair and light skin by the name of Patricia. She asked me if we could talk, and I agreed. We walked towards the entrance of the place where there was a big comfortable bar. She stood next to another young lady and we were introduced.

Patricia introduced me to Ms. Paloma Suau. She told me that Paloma had seen me dancing earlier and asked her to bring me to her and that she wanted to ask me if I would be interested in participating in this project that she was directing. I was given an address, date, and time when I was to meet them, and just like that, without asking or knowing about it, that opportunity came to me. I did not audition; Paloma just wanted to take some pictures and needed me to fill out some forms. On that day, one of the costume makers took my measurements, and somebody took a few videos of me dancing with several other people who were there. After a few weeks, I was with Danny Rivera and other artists inside an old building in Old San Juan, dancing with my partner Otoquí Reyes. I participated in another scene with José Cámara and other talented Bomba dancers and drummers.

It was an interesting experience that I learned so much from. It started easy but slowly became as complicated as any big project can be. As a result of participating in this project, the people who had collaborated for years all of a sudden changed. In retrospect, the attitudes and dramas that occurred because of different issues at the end worked well for all of us. Those challenges that seemed negative at the time became a catalyst for what would happen to Bomba later. I must say that the separations between the Bomba and Plena artists were necessary for the diversification, expansion, and inclusion of new people in the Bomba community.

I think Bomba chose us, and during that time we all played our part to help create a new system that would slowly transform how folklore was looked at. There was a collective need to heal from something, fill a void in our lives, and Bomba showed each of us the way to an individual and collective purpose. I also think Bomba was still in mourning and needed to heal from one of her son's passing. As I had mentioned before, Rafael Cepeda Atiles passed away in 1996, and perhaps those sounds, movements, and life that he had given Bomba needed to survive through Don Rafael's students and family. That force we call Bomba chose to continue in a way that was not controlled by some but was free for everyone to share with her. I believe there was a higher and meaningful purpose behind this sudden artistic movement. Agueybana, CICRE, Son del Batey, Taller Tamboricua, and Yubá Iré, which combined Afro-Cuban genres and Bomba in their repertoire, were some of the first groups to move between traditions and innovations between 1997 and early 2000s to this day. Meanwhile, there were groups doing the same in Mayaguez, Ponce, Añasco, and slowly other towns were opening to this experience. These groups and individuals who were part of the movement created a new energy, and a new way to resist oppression.

We made things easier for future generations because Bomba was easier to learn. There was no need to be a part of a dance company or any strings attached. At the same time, I think we removed something special from it, something ancestral, that was either made up by the families that decided to hold on to Bomba or maybe it was, in fact, a traditional practice that they only knew what they were doing and did not tell us.

Back then, learning Bomba was like a rite of passage. People had to earn their way into the marquesinas of these well-known families. Students had to prove they could be part of their dance companies, not only with talent but also by creating these relationships with their mentors and elders based on trust. Don Rafael Cepeda and Doña Caridad Brenes' children were the ones who held their parent's legacy with care and zealousness during and after their parents' passing. They continued teaching their students to earn the roles they aspired in Bomba as either dancers or drummers.

They taught us, and still do, that people need to work their way up to become a lead dancer or drummer. Only that lovitment (love+commitment) made a good artist. The student needed to know the foundation and develop the skills to have the elders blessing. If someone wanted to do something on their own and wanted to build their legacy, they had to have those things, especially the blessing of the elders and their support to be respected and acknowledged. It was hard work but worth every minute of it. If the objective of our work is to give this art form and history continuity, then it is impossible to do it without the elders, without foundation, and without their validation, because although we are all individuals, we chose to do an art that is about collective experience that depends on the past, it depends on those who were before us, the memories of those who can share that information, and that requires a connection with our elders.

This movement was called Movimiento Bombazo, and I remember that at first everyone felt a bit pressured. Elders felt it was their responsibility to supervise and pay attention to what we were all doing because of a sense of ownership and respect for a legacy that was older than them, and that they had sacrificed so much for. There was a genuine concern for what could happen to Bomba and the uncertainty that this disruption, this new movement that was breaking traditions in some ways, might hurt or deform Bomba. Trust became an issue not only between mentors and former students, but in time also among those who began collaborating with each other's cultural work.

A new Bomba emerged that was not that simple or pretty. Bombazos, which is the word we use to name Bomba parties or performances, became very popular and eventually, our elders began to show up to see what was happening. I remember the first time I saw Modesto Cepeda walking with one of his daughters into Rumba. The look on his face was priceless. The number of people singing and dancing, and the energy was unbelievable. He might not have guessed that this was happening; that we were all doing this to a younger generation that fell in love with it.

Bomba's identity reflected a new representation that also respected the past. Bomba wore jeans, hair in locks, sneakers, and flowy Indian skirts with bareback tops. Bomba's following were college kids, tourists, Puerto Ricans from New York, and people who wanted to have a good time, drink, and listen to live music without the shadow of what it was as a traditional folkloric expression and the history behind costumes. Bomba sounded like a calling, not of resistance, but of inclusion, and it was on stage, on screens, and in a cyber world that Bomba was also branching out. Bomba was seen in all of those ways but we always brought it back to what it was. We made space in our performances to talk about its history.

Bomba emerged in spaces of pain, sadness, and bondage. It also emerged in spaces of sacredness. Rumba and other places became a space for healing and liberation. It was a church to exorcise our oppressed spirits and dance with and for our ancestros, even though those objectives were not articulated as we do now. These were places to go to listen to new chants and new stories. It did not matter if people knew how to dance or not. Everyone could dance off and on stage, learn a step or two, and feel like a star for a few seconds and see some of the local stars of Puerto Rico's backyard and international ones also that happened to visit the island, and joined us, and also danced, played or sang with us.

La tarima, although it became inclusive and many people danced freely and some were applauded for their excellency, while others for bravery and effort, became a place to learn about tolerance and appreciate others' learning process as we slowly forget how we all started. It was a place to look at and reflect on our process as dancers and drummers, and in my case, I was interested in defining how to teach in a different way. We did not want to be judgmental but at the same time, we were all dealing with the ego trips that are part of these experiences. We learned to teach with kindness and flexibility while we still struggled with the old ways. In my days I learned Bomba differently. Our mentors demanded perfection like any dance company requires from their dancers. Bomba dance companies, which in fact originally were only two of them, and later others were started, did not have to be any different from other dance genres, because the main goal was and continues to be a performative and for that people need to be ready and master the skills required to deliver a good performance.

Our mentors put us through rigorous training and hours of learning until students went beyond knowing how to dance and drum. They prepared their students to become Bomba. At least that was how I was taught, and I believe the same of the group of people I know as Bomberos de la mata, a phrase that refers to authenticity and expertise. It was in Bomba dance circles where you separated la paja del trigo, meaning the experienced dancers from the rest, and back then, for some, el trigo were mentored by a Cepeda.

Most of the people who danced on stage in Rumba knew what they were doing, and without giving a formal class, while having fun, they were also teaching others. The sidewalk in front of Rumba's entrance was like a red carpet for the avant-garde Bomba artists. People struggled to find parking and walked up Old San Juan Hills to get there early and stand close to the stage. Anyone who was anybody in Bomba went there and danced to the son of the Batey that Omar "Pipo" Sánchez and other members of the group created. We kept the essence and removed the theatrical Eurocentric aesthetic that represented and romanticized oppression and colonization.

Me revestí with bright colors during a Bomba renaissance that became an act of remembrance and history in the making. We incorporated ourselves into Bomba's history, and with that, we created a contemporary Afro-Puerto Rican history that we are still working on. In the act of resisting, reclaiming, and reaffirming, we have contributed with new narratives that matter because Bomba has played a role in Puerto Rican identity. Neo Bomba became transnational, and with that, we include ourselves in an Afro-diasporic history in the United States. I traveled with Bomba and met people who liked how the music moved me and how I moved the skirt. Those moves had stories to share, and I never left my elders out of them. Again, life and Bomba wanted me to move, so I grabbed my skirt and went to different stages where Bomba mixed harmoniously with Salsa music, Jazz, and Classical music with Opera singers. All of a sudden it was Bomba con to'. Bomba with Hip Hop, Poetry, Flamenco. You name it, I did it and loved it because Bomba and I became diverse while living in La *100 x 35.*

In the middle of that evolution, I was ready to create something new besides my dance. I supported every idea of mixing the old with the new, tradition with contemporary, Boricua with my Nuyorican identity and doing what felt good and aligned with my standards. I moved around with what was a part of me. I included my son, my experiences, my dreams. I moved with faith, the trust that my elders had in me, and the wings that Bomba gifted me with. I also had an experience of blackness and African-American culture that always made me do things differently.

El Movimiento Bombazo in Puerto Rico created the formula for the Bomba of the Diaspora. This movement originated from a handful of people who also took risks, learned from their elders in Casitas, and they too invested time, learned from elders, and dusted off la estampa de la Bomba, making her resilient to cold weather, aggressive, and raw.

Both of these movements helped build a cultural bridge where Nuyoricans visited the island and learned from Puerto Rico, while people went to New York City to do the same. An exchange of information, artists, and styles created a collaborative Bomba where different meanings of Puerto Ricaness were danced and drummed. Bomberos like Juan Usera, Alex LaSalle, Tato Torres, and others, were known in the Bomba scene. Places like Rumba, Camaradas, Nuyorican Café, Nuyorican Poets Café, and others were our platforms. Bigger groups like Los Pleneros de la 21 were rewriting Bomba's history alongside the Bomba institutions where we learned from. It is a never-ending task, like a conjure that has made us pledge allegiance to a sound and the movements that tell ancestral stories that nobody can really decipher. Our mission is to heal, to move, to progress in ways that we ground ourselves as we invite others to join us without oppressing anyone, or at least that is not supposed to happen. We remember where we came from, what has given us an identity to know who we are and where we need to go. Revestida, dressed with a divine luster, I move to make Bomba shine and she shares her light with all of her children.

Revestida la Bomba va desde aquel tiempo. Revestidos iban jóvenes y nuestros mayores hacia la evolución. Revestidas íbamos la Bomba y yo por la encendida calle antillana del Viejo San Juan. Calles adoquinadas llenas de ecos de zaguanes y hogares de sanjuaneros en resistencia al cambio de su pueblo, a no dejar el control, ni la blancura de su ciudad amurallada. Invasión de carros modernos buscando espacio. El parqueo, pa'l jangueo, dejando a los caballos descansar en lo que a la Bomba se iba a gozar, beber, conocer gente nueva y darse a conocer. Revestidas de Valija Gitana y faldas que fueron estrechándose cada vez más hasta terminar en estolas de españolas arrepentidas de haber llegado a un puerto caluroso que tapaba sus cuerpos ibéricos. Revestidas íbamos de escotes, pelos alterados por el salitre, bembas con brillos y delineadores que guían la mirada hacia el amor, la desconfianza, el sonido, y tambores que suenan su invitación. Revestida de ciudad, del área metro, de rebeldía, juventud, y tradición que se ajusta y adapta porque sino muere. Revestidos todos con Bomba en mano a cambiar al mundo, a Macondo, a la juventud, nuestra historia y a un-Puerto con todos sus negros, sus cocólos de caras amulatadas que culipandeando van en tacones por las calles de la ciudad. Por ahí va, la Bomba que a todos llama. Gracias a todos, todas, todx por tantas memorias bonitas. Eso es lo único que nos llevaremos y cuando llegue el momento, revestidos de nuestras glorias en algún batey celestial nos veremos.

Part 10

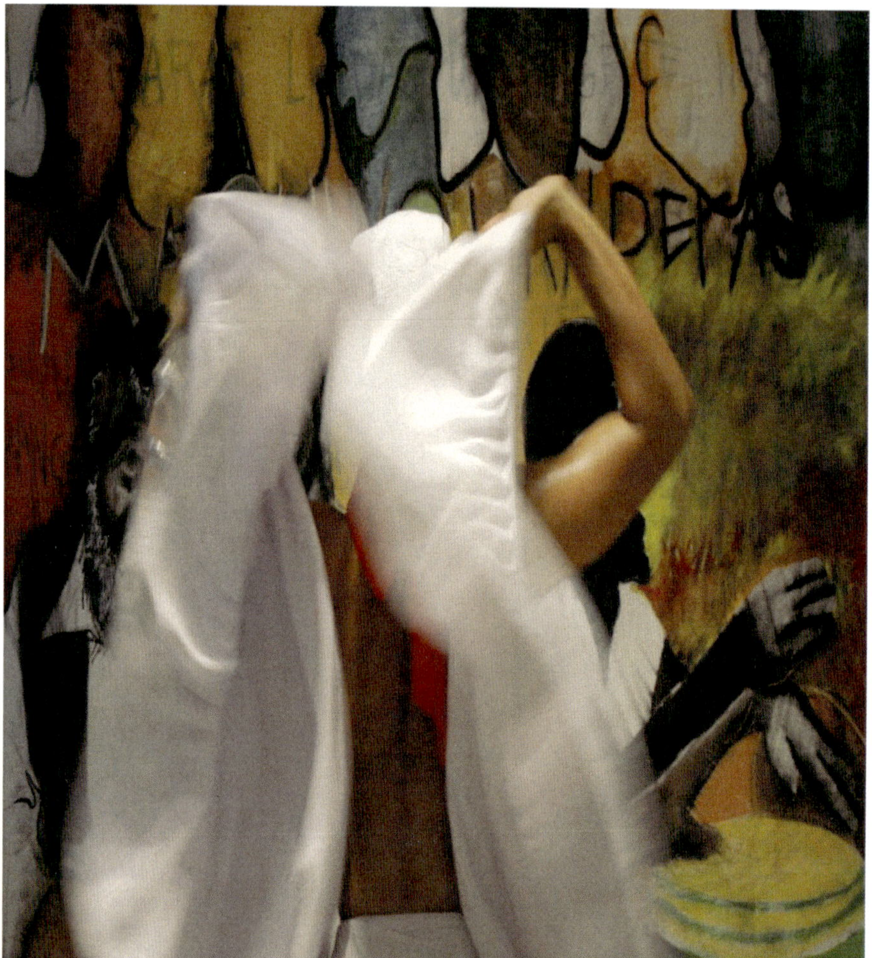

Bomba Gives you Wings

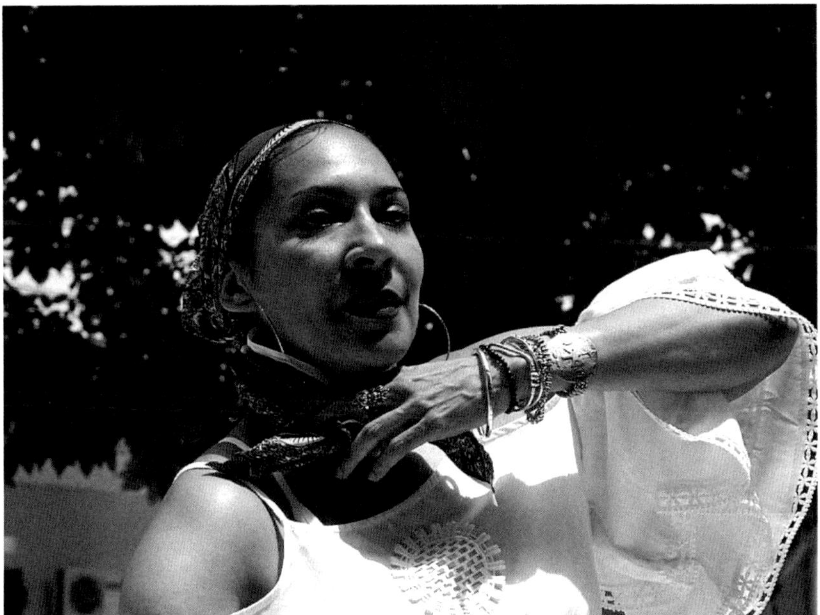

Photograph by Cuban artist: Olaph Johe Quiala

Bomba gave me wings, and I flew

I danced before I learned to dance Bomba. Bomba was not the first music I heard nor the first music I danced to, and dancing was one of the rituals that brought my family together. We all respond to sounds before we learn to walk, and for some, when we learn how to dance, we can fly. When learning to dance, the person begins to understand how to move in particular ways and gains awareness of the feeling of freedom of movement. That kinetic knowledge can be transferred to other life activities and for dancers it changes the way they walk, and also the way they use a prop. Even in their stillness you can see that the body has been trained differently. Artists gesticulate in ways that can make nonverbal communication more interesting than words can ever express. The Bomba cultural movement I chose to join created different options for representation and movement, and the embodied cultural information, the past, traumas, and need for release, continued changing the dance. In Bomba, the skirt has been one of the things that has transcended time.

To dance Bomba with a skirt, the dancer requires a level of mastery that takes time and patience to develop. My experience with the skirt is a loving one. The skirt became my wings and gave my body and energy a larger reach. It makes me feel the same feeling of exhilaration than when I used to get on a swing when I was a kid. Dancing has taught me the groundedness and technique to apply to life's ups and downs, making me steady and centered, but the skirt has helped me fly and flow through it, and throughout my dance journey, it has lifted me and has been my companion to this day.

My skirt created an image for me that defined me as a dancer, and my identity as a woman in this artistry to a certain extent. The way my mentors taught me how to use it, has made a huge difference in the way that I dance. The skirt has matured with me. There is nothing as beautiful to me as the effect and volume that a skirt creates when the dancer knows how to manage it. To master it, the dancer needs to know how the body needs to move to create the desired effect, and therefore, it is the understanding of movement what is really important. Los líos de faldas en la Bomba can be interpreted in many ways, and dancing with one is one of them. The grace in the dance depends on how well a person feels, and understands how to flow with the skirt, how to hold it, and knowing what fabric and weight is the proper one for a person to dance comfortably in, among other details. A skirt is supposed to be an extension of the dancers' upper extremities.

My first skirt only had five yards of fabric; that was the standard amount of fabric needed. Eventually, that increased, and the fabric and designs changed too. The first person to change the skirt's traditional style that I know of was Tata Cepeda. From using cotton fabric, the Bomba skirt changed to rayon blends, and other very expensive fabrics that also added weight. Suddenly, the styles and cuts were different, and from five yards, the skirts had eight, ten, or more yards of fabric.

I have tried them all, and each style of the skirt also changes the dance, but the purpose is the same. The purpose of my skirts has been to create a musical voice, a means to collaborate in the creation of sounds, a teaching tool, a prop to beautify a stage and performance, and an aesthetic piece that beautifies my body while telling a story of feelings.

When I was a kid, I fell in love with yards of fabric, which inspired me to pursue an art that marked my life. The skirt eventually holds a sentimental value that comes out in my dance. In my opinion, not everyone looks graceful dancing with one, and they would do much better focusing on footwork and gestures if they knew how to, or had a good dance instructor to teach them. One of the objectives of the Bombazo movement was to find the middle ground between tradition and contemporary expressions, which was reflected in the dance as well. I saw the evolution of the dance as things progressed, and although we were all for change, the skirt was that item that connected the past with the present in the dance, and we all agreed to keep it. In this movement the skirt also evolved and some dancers have evolved too.

The Bomba skirt is a muse that, as a protagonist in Bomba dance, was meant to conceal, decorate, contain, express something, and identify a body and a specific gender. The skirt survived with the drums as part of those Caribbean objects connected to a diasporic, creole sociocultural, and artistic expression. This prop has a social and historical meaning worth reviewing. It is an instrument that has established social values and broken cultural traditions. As a means to knowledge, art, and history, the Bomba skirt has helped transition the cultural and social values of women from an epoch of silence and demure to becoming a tool to express a voice for more outspoken, modern, and active women that did not mind using it to create a more challenging Bomba dance. Women also created musical challenges while claiming a space in circles where traditionally, men were in charge.

Although dance steps are just movements within structures of rhythm, and other factors that define them or give them value, dance steps have also been categorized and used to distinguish gender when teaching these dances. Folkloric art is meant to keep a tradition that shows the socio-cultural values of a specific time in history, and although we continue evolving while practicing these folkloric expressions, we need to remember that these art forms are meant to preserve cultural, social, and moral traditions. The teaching of Bomba dance has been structured in a way that categorizes specific steps or movements based on two main identities, which are what we know today as cis men and cis women. There was no space for switching roles, unless it was a carnival where these expressions were just role play and not meant to be a real thing, even if we all know that reality was different.

This structure is based on the traditional values and representation of these genders from back in the day. Men's traditional Bomba dance has not changed much. Men's dance has always been characterized by footwork with interesting patterns, figures, and, of course, ingenuity that might create a new style that can be described as aggressive, agile, elegant, or paused and daring at times. All of these movements happen during the improvisation. Meanwhile, for women, Bomba dance has changed significantly. Among all my mentors, Margarita Sánchez Cepeda aka Tata Cepeda was one of the women who polished my skills. Tata taught me during a time in her life when she wanted to teach and share what she knew in the way she understood it, which was not necessarily how she learned it. Her style of teaching was in many ways different than what others were doing, including members of her family. I will dare to say that it was different than the way she teaches now. My experience with her was a one-on-one, intense session that was not planned to be that way; it just happened. I also had the desire and time to learn, not really to learn the dance, but to understand what happens while dancing and creating a composition. I wanted to understand what was the motivation and the energy behind the movement, and find out what that looked and felt like in me. Anyone can imitate, but that wasn't what I wanted to do nor what Tata wanted from me either. I already danced with Modesto and to dance a choreography is not challenging when you know how to dance, but to dance Bomba is something else, and requires skills that not many get to develop properly.

During the limited time we were able to share, I felt that explosion in me. I felt something click but like a diamond, it happened under pressure. I will always respect and appreciate the time she dedicated me. Tata Cepeda added something special to the new Bomba movement that had emerged. She contributed with the design of her skirts, and new dance movements that mixed a flamenco style that I also had the opportunity to share with her when she began learning to dance Sevillana. The extra fabric that she added to her skirts enabled her to extend her arms up higher and avoided pulling the fabric, which might have been very uncomfortable and unattractive. She created a different style and became *La Mariposa de la Bomba*. Tata also changed the color schemes that were traditionally used in Bomba skirts, and even inspired other women to sew Bomba skirts like hers.

When I think of our time together, and seeing how her dance changed in the process, I understand that every person's interpretation of their dance represents them, and these are never the same as our bodies, our mobility, and understanding changes. The body, the cognitive and emotional understanding of movement, music, and the relationship that one creates with a prop will define a particular style, and reflect the uniqueness of that body in motion. But the main purpose of Bomba dance, and all of the knowledge acquired in the process, is to say something, and that message needs to be musically in tune with many other elements, and also unique. The purpose of teaching someone to dance is not to make them end up looking like the instructor; it is to help them express themselves fully by encouraging the student to use their body, and abilities to the fullest in the ways that are particular to that body, the person's personality, and authentic ways of expression. Even if there are people really good at imitating, a person's essence is a part of the whole dance experience, and that cannot be taken from another individual. This authentic expression will also help create a musical, and corporeal Bomba language where the skirt plays a role in composing, and it has to be done with style, musically, and in movement.

The Bomba skirt is an iconic tool that mesmerized me and shaped my dance. I have learned to respect and admire its power because it keeps transforming its purpose, reaching out to impact more people, and tearing down social norms that continue to hide under it. Each undulation and manipulation of this prop has also changed the narrative of gender, and has created options for people who want to experiment with it and dance without it. It has created a broader way of interacting with the Bomba drum and improvising. The skirt has not only impacted Bomba dance and music, it has also impacted the Bomba community by creating inclusivity, and sometimes even resentments. Biological men who choose to dance with a skirt have taken it from women to create their dance and reaffirm a gender identity that is nontraditional. Historically, in many cultures, men have always taken the places, and spaces of women in the arts, especially in dance and theater. Men dressed up as women to do theater, dance as geishas, and do other dances where they wore costumes and makeup to perform as women, because women were not allowed by men to be in those spaces and practice those art disciplines.

Women have struggled to be a part of the performative art world in many societies. The appropriation of women's identity, image, and movements is not new. Although in contemporary dance, men were already wearing skirts as a performative and experimental prop, in most Caribbean folk dances, this was not seen or acceptable because of the purpose of folkloric artistic traditions, and also back then Bomba groups were made up of families and controlled by them.

Bomba groups were represented by families with their moral codes and social pressures that were interposed. There are many cultures where men wear long robes and kilts and are accepted, and the people understand the meaning, but in Puerto Rico, that was not the case. The Bomba skirt was worn by women only. In time, it was shared with some resistance and in sharing it, women revised how the men that choose to wear it dance with it, look with it, and how their movements slowly create a different style because it is, after all, a male body in motion regardless of gender identity issues. Whether taking the skirt off or putting it on, the skirt has made a very important statement in society. It has made an impact not only in the dance but also in the body that dances and has challenged the social expectations of who is entitled to wear it.

I am not saying that I disagree or that I am okay with it. What I do believe is that because art is fluid, then as such, it should meet the needs of the artist. What I know because I have experienced it, is that women, black women, are always struggling to find safe spaces and have fewer opportunities for artistic and social representation than men in many areas. There are also disparities between men and women that need to be addressed in the arts as well. In a patriarchal society with systems that are entitled to determine what things can represent women, and how we are supposed to represent ourselves, including what we do with our bodies, we need to understand that the skirt is one of those things that some women hold on to because of its personal meaning, and how it facilitates the ways they can express themselves as who they are. I strongly believe that the Bomba skirt became a part of a feminist movement that also gave them a musical voice that with time, has become louder and stronger. When I mention the idea of a feminist movement, I am referring to how little things, little actions, can have a huge impact, and without being explicit about it, it still creates change.

While in other social manifestations of feminist movements, the pants became their symbol, in Bomba, the skirt became powerful thanks to those pioneers who started using the skirt in a different way, changing their dance and, therefore, the drumming, and vice versa.

With the evolution of this prop as a feminist and female voice, something else happened. Women's Bomba dance shifted from being represented by a skirt to being represented by drumming. I was a part of both, and although I began that drumming revolution in Puerto Rico with a group of women who agreed to embark on that risky mission in the year 2005, the skirt movement was strong, and was what I identified the most with as a dancer. I was pushed by Bomba to plant a seed of my own evolution, and I did it on my terms in the dance and also the music.

While in Puerto Rico, we clung to our skirts, in NYC, there has always been a tendency to dance without one. I think that the reason is that some elders in the community who began teaching back in the day taught the Loiza style to improvise. Also, men were at the forefront of teaching young kids, boys and girls, to dance Bomba.

In my travels to and from New York, I have danced with skirts, fans, scarves, and anything pretty that I could manipulate because if you know how to dance with a skirt, you will know how to manipulate anything. But to my taste, I have always preferred to use a skirt, and it became my trademark as a dancer. A skirt in motion is beautiful to look at, and for a Bomba connoisseur, you can tell the skill level of a dancer not only in manipulating a skirt in their dance but, most importantly, in creating music with the necessary precision while using it. Moving skirts have inspired painters and visual artists who find in their images patterns that become art that lasts seconds in midair, and a lifetime in a painting or sculpture. The Bomba skirt also influenced the way I dressed because, as an artist, my Bomba skirt was part of my whole attire. It was not just about being on stage anymore, or choosing whether to wear a costume or not; it was about personal taste and style.

My Bomba skirt became a part of the regular night-out wardrobe, whether it was for performing or hanging out. Seamstresses were in demand because dancers wanted skirts in different colors, textures, and styles that looked good on their bodies. Every aspect of Bomba was influencing one another and creating a domino effect. One movement led to another, and the way dance changed required an adjustment to the skirt. Larger movements required more fabric, and more fabric required more skills; for a seamstress meant more work, and for dancers, new ways to create. I supported the idea of refusing to use traditional Bomba costumes to perform and kept the skirt, because although I still find traditional attires beautiful, I understood that the narrative had to change. As much as I missed the whole ritual of putting on layers of clothes to become a depiction of a woman of the XVI century, I knew the costume also had another meaning, and to reach younger generations, some things needed to look different, including myself.

In Puerto Rico, there aren't many rites of passage for youth, and belonging to a dance company is one of the ways of living this experience. To belong to a dance company means that the dancer has earned that position, and to finally dress up is like a ritual. Having the dress made, fitted, and finally dressing up to go on stage, for many becomes a rite of passage and something earned. Being a member of a Bomba dance company or any dance company requires long hours of training, and working your way to a spot of visibility, and depending on how good the dancer is, the dancer can become a leader in the group. Dressing up means having a certain status, and it was then that students became performers. As I mentioned before, I come from a time when the status you had was given by an elder, and the student worked for it. The elder introduced you to the community, and the elder's name and acknowledgment was your presentation card to show in other respectable spaces, and for other people to recognize you as part of the community. There was pride in saying, "I came from X family, or I performed with this or that family", and the anecdotes that are part of the whole performative experience, and dressing up is one of them. Dressing up becomes a ritual of belonging, a ritual of representation of Puerto Rican black people, which is significant not only for the artist but also for the spectator.

When women get together in a dressing room, a tent, and sometimes even outdoors in the open with other women covering one another to dress up for a performance, it becomes an opportunity to learn and bond. Mentors teach tricks and techniques to fix a headwrap and fix last-minute clothes malfunctions. Women share anecdotes and prayers before the performance to relax and support one another. The dress down is also a ritual of returning to self, which creates a certain emotion that can be hard to detach from right away. It is a feeling of sudden emptiness that does not last long, but it is felt nonetheless. I remember observing how little girls were all excited because they wore makeup just for the occasion. Behind the historical and racial meaning of the traditional Bomba costume, there are many beautiful stories of Puerto Rican black life and how these families provided young black Puerto Rican kids an opportunity to experience that artistic life that otherwise might have been impossible. Young people have traveled to other parts of the world with these groups and feel they are part of something grand.

Through the art of Bomba, many empowering things happen to Youth and children despite the different ways of interpreting the meaning of a costume. It required a great deal of love and commitment, especially when performing under hot stage lights or the blazing sun, ready to pass out while drums are reminding you to keep going. I am not going to lie; I was more than happy to let go and only keep my skirts to dance with. I knew that I had to let go, not only because of my comfort but also because I had to change the affixed ideas of racism that the traditional Bomba costume carries. There is a historical significance in these costumes that continues to romanticize colonization and slavery. I used those dresses plenty of times without thinking about how the image perpetuates a narrative that does not help younger generations to break away from the prejudice and negativity towards black people in our history. I enjoy the theatrics in the performing experience, but spectators leave with images that are attached to information that is connected to cultural, racial, and social meanings.

Those dresses made me fall in love with Bomba when I was a kid, and I still miss them sometimes, but with time I understood how I had to create a new image, a new narrative, and support a new movement. I have also seen how costumes stand out and make performances look better than Bomba groups wearing regular, modern fashions. I believe that performer in regular clothing need to be spectacular because if not, then it ends up being a plain, unattractive presentation.

As an educator, I believe I have the responsibility of questioning the impact of the different resources I use to share information and also knowing when they work for or against my objectives as an artist, a woman, and a free thinker. If my work is not causing a positive change then I need to pause to reflect, and adjust. It is my responsibility to be aware of how I am doing things, remove myself from narratives that are scripted and damaging, and create stereotypes that misrepresents me and what I believe in. I chose to liberate my body from layers of complex historical information that hide my identity in the hope of creating a moment, just a moment of the spectator's attention, to make a connection. The connection to the present, a moment to create a memory for us while they see me. A woman of African descent who shares the past in a different way. In the ways that are felt, heard, and not only seen. I want to create a possibility of a new form of representation and expression, where I celebrate who I am as a woman, with my skirt, as an artist that enjoys the body where my spirit resides, and shares that joy and gratitude through movement. I carry that foundation in me, I am those traditions that are also flexible and shares spaces with other skirts that tell other stories. I chose to represent my history in a way that also liberates me and helps me move easier, wider, higher, and fly to places where I meet the past and bring it to life.

Part 11

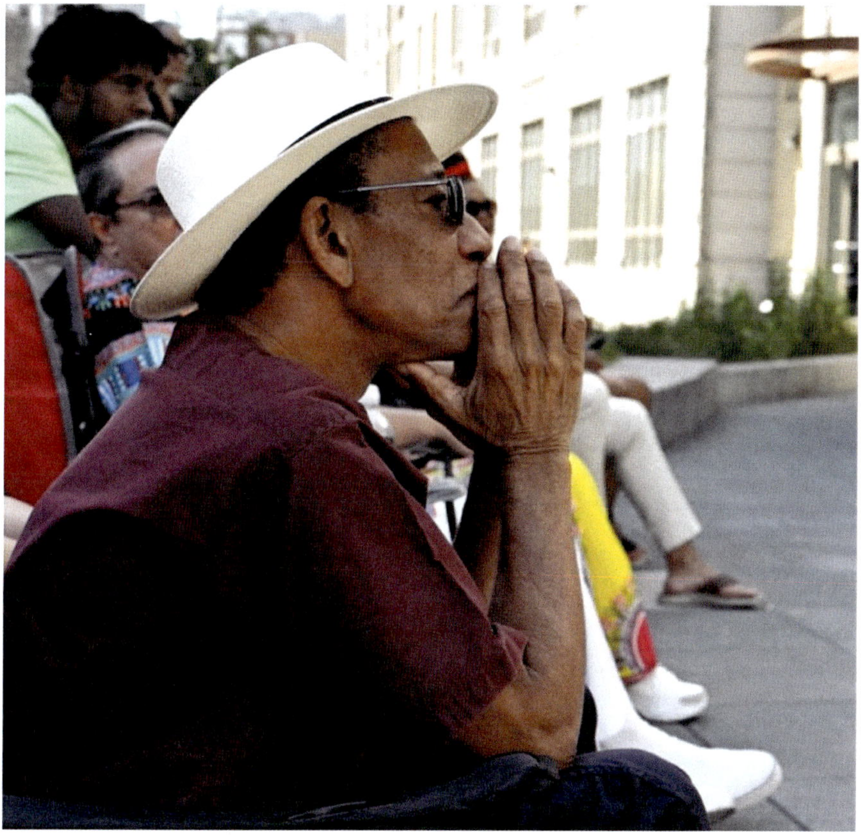

Coffee with Jesus

Coffee with Jesus

Jesús Manuel, toca mi Bomba, toca mi Bomba, Jesús Manuel ponte a tocar mi balancé. Balancé, balance, aquél que encontramos, el que debemos de crear, el que lo establece en la música y el baile de Bomba.

Many people love Bomba, but very few put in the work to learn enough to be able to teach or perform it correctly. The group of people that can do the work is relatively small in comparison to the people that attend Bombazos. Now, people teach Bomba to everyone and everywhere, but back then, it was not like that. Ownership has been something instilled by the families that have taught us, and it was for a reason. These families kept a tight grip on Bomba, whom they allowed into their homes, and sometimes it felt they also controlled their students, or so it seemed at times. I believe this controlling behavior was out of a sense of safety and because they saw their students as an extended family with whom they had shared something valuable with. They shared their life's work with their students and also a space in their homes. There is a collection of notebooks written by Don Rafael Cepeda with Bomba songs and anecdotes of what Santurce was like back in the day, the way of life, and the people that were part of an Afro-Puerto Rican culture that are documented in these journals. For the Cepeda Family, Don Rafael's work is their inheritance, and ours.

Becoming a Bombero meant becoming a guardian of our black ancestry. A custodian of a legacy, of our art, and all the other secrets that they kept as a way for their survival. Back in my elders' days, the only ones who valued Bomba were black people. For black people it was a safe community to share and practice a form of spirituality, which does not have to do with religion. To enter these homes and become a member of that community (family), you really must have had the acceptance and esteem from an elder or someone they trusted that put in a good word for you. To this day, a lot of people say: "La Bomba de los Cepeda, de los Ayala, de los Alduen, and other families that, even though they did not own it, they worked hard to keep that legacy alive, and earned that position of leadership.

Many families in Puerto Rico and the children of those elders remember what it was to feel hungry, lacking basic things, and the types of work that men and women had to do to earn an honest living. A lot of black grandmothers worked as maids, nannies, or cooked for white people in Puerto Rico. Slavery evolved, and black Puerto Ricans, especially on the coast, lived in poverty, and unfortunately poverty also became a legacy. The idea of owning something gives a sense of power and entitlement over it. It also impacts identity. Bomba was one of the very few things black people owned. The reason why it was important to learn from these elders was that they were la cepa de donde vienes. They were the real OG's. They were the ones who prepared you and helped you master a skill that guaranteed them that the student would be able to represent them with honor, and also represent the house where you were taught, while preserving this art.

To do Bomba back then was harder, but to keep it was way easier than today because it was a black thing, and nobody wanted it, the ones who did did not have competition, and it was a part of a daily life that had not gained the popularity or status that it has today. Era "una cosa de negros" that dragged the stigma of slavery. A lot of people enjoyed it, but like we say, de afuerita, as outsiders and not mingling too much or at all with the crowd of black people. It was a moment to let lo de negra o negro salir pa' fuera, or to let something get into the person that made them dance. Moments where the black grandmother hidden in the closet came out and reminded the light skinned person who forgot about their ancestry, to do a reality check.

Whoever walks into this way of art and life, this way of doing community and healing should do it with the honesty of their biases and a clear concept of who they are. They should be mindful of treating people, spaces, and Bomba with respect, not by ignoring its roots and reality, not by generalizing for their own benefit and just labeling it Puerto Rican and dismissing the fact that it was not the backs of white people who got lashed or were punished for drumming, but rather facing it and looking at its people up close. Looking closely at its stories of survival, suffering, liberation, and how black people had to fight to keep this. It is important to look at its blackness as a gift that represents our motherland, the real one, where the mother of humankind resides because, we are able to do what we do because others sacrificed a great deal for the preservation of this. In the words of Don Rafael Cepeda, which his son Jesús shared with me: "Yo me he jodido mucho por defender esto." Therefore, we cannot ignore that when we talk about this and decide to be a part of other people's stories.

Life brings people together in different spaces and I was able to meet with a Bomba elder in The Bay area in San Francisco, that I already knew, but in this particular time we had the time and privacy to talk without rushing, while enjoying a cup of coffee. I met with Denise Solis first, the director of Taller Tambó, and of many other cultural projects that date back to 2007 in the state of California. We both met with Jesús Cepeda in her house.

I had coffee with Jesus. El maestro Don Jesús Manuel Cepeda Brenes, son of Don Rafael Cepeda and Doña Caridad Brenes. Not only is he a great musician, an important Bomba elder, and a steward of his parent's legacy, this man is also a great storyteller. We walked into a cozy kitchen where a small table invited us to sit and get comfortable. Denise offered to make some coffee, and like good Puerto Ricans, we did not refuse the offer. It was an opportunity to talk about anything and something we all had in common—Bomba. As we waited for the coffee to be done, we began talking about what we had done and how things were going. Jesús has a peculiar and unique way of talking that adds a touch of humor to everything. When he sat, he crossed his legs, and his pose was relaxed, elegant, and familiar. He is easy to talk with, loves life and music, and is passionate about his culture and Puerto Rico. He loves his family and admires his father and the work his family has done for so many years. That legacy, although it is a reason to feel pride, has made him humble, curious to learn and explore new things, open to sharing with others; supportive, and willing to share a lifetime of experience in his trade to help others who are committed to doing Bomba responsibly, with love, and respect.

Denise wanted him to eat something, so she wanted to cook before we headed out to a concert that she had invited us to. As we waited for the coffee and he was talking, I observed his hands, his gestures, and his facial expressions. I could not help but wonder how a man like that, who breathes Bomba and has done it all his life, would define what Bomba meant for him. I thought about asking him because everyone knows the textbook definition, but after all, he is the son of Rafael Cepeda, and I was sure his definition was going to make my day, so I asked him. Denise served us coffee, and as I sat facing him and continued prepping his meal, he heard my question and took a sip of his coffee. His look changed. The whole vibe changed, or at least that was what I perceived. There was a solemnity that deserved attention and respect. He focused his eyes on something or perhaps nothing, but I knew he went into a space that I was familiar with. A space where my family would go to all the time when they thought about something important, something worth analyzing and explaining with calmness. He spoke in the same way my elders did. A space where memories, wisdom, spirits, dreams, and ancestors live.

Don Jesús paused, and at the same time was sure about what he was going to say. He spoke with a soft tone, a clear voice, and a pride that was earned and at the same time instilled in him by his family. He said in his deep voice to me and Denise, although she was busy doing something else, I know she was listening attentively: - "Para *mi la Bomba es música comunal con raíces. Nosotros somos recipientes de ése género. Es parte de la cultura de un pueblo que ha luchado dentro de las situaciones de la esclavitud de africanos y dentro de su condición para preservar sus conocimientos. Y a pesar de las influencias de otras etnias se cultivó esto (refiriéndose a la Bomba). He continued saying: - "Papi, me definió como Bomba, el nombre con que se define ése género. Esto se respeta, divierte y a la vez ayuda a entrar en una amistad y desarrollo de emociones y amor por la música y la patria."* He took another sip of his coffee and so did I. Denise and I knew that schooling had begun.

One thing took me to the next. I followed by asking if he believed that Bomba has evolved, and if so, how? I wanted to know his opinion because I know things have changed but wanted to confirm if we coincided, which he replied - *"Bomba es un modo de vida y en su desarrollo también se ha convertido en una industria que le dá trabajo a otras personas. Siempre hay una inversión que hacer. Se ha convertido en un negocio que le da de comer a mucha gente, lo único es que debe haber un orden para preservarla y que todos se beneficien. Como la Bomba se ha convertido en un producto que se compra, hay que dar un buen producto, por que están los que aman la cultura y hacen las cosas por amor a la Bomba y a la cultura, y otros que están por ellos mismos, pa' que los vean en una tarima, y entonces están los que hacen cosas por joder, y en todo esto hay una responsabilidad. Ha habido un crecimiento en comparación con los tiempos de antes. Hoy día hay más grupos y sigue entrando gente a esta industria del género de la Bomba y la Plena en comparación con la música jíbara. La Bomba ha logrado superarse y otros géneros la apoyan y buscan identificarse con la música típica como lo han hecho: JLo, Marc Anthony, Ricky Martin, Paul Simon, Eddie Palmieri y otros. Yo recuerdo que en 1973 Jerry Massuchi hizo grabaciones con Bomba y Plena. En ése tiempo había que grabar música típica por que era parte de contratos donde tenían que incluir música autóctona. Jerry Masuchi veía la música de Puerto Rico como algo valioso y eso nos ayudó y ayudó mucho al género. A la Bomba se le ha dado un respeto. La misión de cada persona que se meta en esto es seguir trabajando unidos para dejar algo para el futuro de los que vienen atrás."*

I felt good to listen to his opinion which I agreed and to know that we shared the same observations because, after all, I learned with them. He continued talking without rushing and seemed very comfortable. Maybe talking about Bomba made him feel at home. I wrote as fast and accurately as I could because I did not want to leave anything out, and I wanted to write exactly what he was saying. It was not my intention to have the conversation we were having, and I was not prepared with questions or devices. I even forgot about my phone. It just happened, just a flow of thoughts that created a beautiful conversation. It was a natural moment, and the natural thing for me to do was to write. I am sharing his message with you while I get to cherish those same words pronounced in his raspy voice.

That also reminded me of a time when a lot of people came from the United States to visit Bomba elders to do research and interview them. I also remember when the "Bombazo" movement started and how there was a bit of tension or a little resistance on both parts.

Sometimes, due to a lack of understanding about what Bomba must have meant for these families that became cultural agencies, part of Puerto Rican cultural tradition and representatives of our folklore. In this collective mission, people forget how hard it must have been to share Bomba with people who moved on after getting what they wanted, and although it might have helped Bomba in a greater sense, it was not fair to the families, and people they used.

Bomba finds us, or we find it at different stages in our lives, and for our elders, Bomba was not about hype, social media attention, and performance. Many Puerto Rican black people lived in poverty, and their quality of life was not the best. The opportunities to have a good job, finish school or even go to school were limited. Back in their day, other values helped communities survive. People helped each other, and there was a tribal mentality of collective welfare and reciprocity. People shared food, watched each other's children, and knew what was happening in their communal spaces. They might have been poor but had a different type of richness that made up for whatever they lacked. Bomba became, for many families, a way of sustainability. The stories that Don Jesús shared that I did not include them in this work, gave me a glimpse of how hard it was for them to make ends meet. The sacrifices that Don Rafael Cepeda, his wife, and his children made for others to enjoy the privilege of knowing Bomba and doing Bomba. It is not the same thing to have a steady job, a comfortable home, live in abundance, and one day wake up and choose to do Bomba rather than drumming and dancing to eat, and keep a roof over your head and shoes on your feet because there aren't a lot of options. People need to understand the value of what is now a "Hype" for our elders. The narrative of inclusiveness can sometimes fog the truth and take away the historical contributions of black people in Puerto Rico. The resistance or zealousness with which this genre has been guarded is simply because it did not belong to everyone, and those who wanted it worked hard for it. You had to be invited. Bomba chose you, and an elder had to guide you, which is very different than what is happening today. Like Don Jesús said, it is an industry and like everything made "Al por mayor" not necessarily the quality is the best. I know it might sound harsh or arrogant, but I would not be honest if I kept my opinion for the sake of not hurting people's sensibility. There is much more to doing this than what people imagine. The hardship that people go through to establish a precedent and the time and investment people make to earn their way to be considered a connoisseur are some of the things that are overlooked when it comes to this art. Without the past, without the foundation and the proper attitude, Bomba will lose a very important thing, and that is its essence and purpose.

Don Jesús Cepeda watched his family struggle. He was a member of a big family in the middle of challenging times in Puerto Rico. It was also a time of political tension. To play Bomba and keep the tradition alive meant running the risk of being imprisoned or harassed. Puerto Rico was in a cultural limbo due to political policies imposed by the United States with the support of Puerto Rican politicians who were sellouts to me. While Puerto Ricans were silenced, in other places like Cuba, and in the United States, African Americans and Puerto Ricans were claiming what was theirs: a piece of land, their sovereignty, and their culture. Puerto Rico was not exempt from wanting and trying to become independent, and the nationalist party tried hard to join the movement. Many people, including my aunt Olga, remembered violent things that happened when the nationalist party attempted to take over. She recalled being a child and walking from school when Vidal Santiago Diaz, a close friend of Don Pedro Albizu Campos, was killed, and suddenly that street became a murder scene. She recalled her teacher running out and trying to get as many kids as she could back into the school because people did not know what was going on, but they heard the shots and feared for their lives. Don Jesús also recalled Cuba's revolution and how that created panic on the island. Those were times of division between those who felt fear and the fearless who were tired of oppression and hunger. Jesús recalled other facts about Puerto Rico during his youth and how the environment influenced him. I wanted to know what things he might have remembered while growing up. We switched from coffee to some fried plantains that Denise made and continued our conversation.

I asked him how it was back then. He shared interesting memories that continued putting things in perspective. His mood changed slowly from the moment of the first question. There was a certain excitement in his eyes. I could tell he went to a happy place. He told me: -*"A mi siempre me gustó la Rumba. Ese género llegó a Puerto Rico con los primeros inmigrantes cubanos que se empezaron a establecer en Puerto Rico. Algunos tenían dinero, otros llegaron con su cultura y su religión. La Rumba empezó a sonar en la calles del barrio, y yo estaba aprendiendo. A mi me gustaba esa jodienda, me gustaba tocarla y meterle. Eso me llamaba y la calle también, y Papi me tenía el ojo puesto. En esos tiempos la televisión era una novedad y Puerto Rico aprovechó la oportunidad que vinieron ingenieros cubanos y usaron ese conocimiento para mejorar la programación de nuestra televisión puertorriqueña. -"*

He kept talking about how much he liked Rumba and a lot of people started learning when Cubans playing in Puerto Rican streets. He also recalled being picked up in school one day by his father and his brother Carlos when the Cuban revolution exploded. They were scared of the repercussions it would have on the island given that in Puerto Rico in the 1950s, the Puerto Rican Nationalist Party had already been in charge of various uprisings known as the Puerto Rican Nationalists Party Revolts of the 50s. Don Jesús mentioned El Maestro, Don Pedro Albizu Campos, and others who were part of the conversations that took place in the community. Puerto Rico, like Cuba, was also going through a political attempt to obtain independence. Puerto Rico had a gag law that began in 1948 and lasted up to 1957. This was imposed by the Puerto Rican Senate, which was controlled by Luis Muñoz Marín. But in rice and beans, as they say in Puerto Rico, what this meant was that it was illegal to display any "Puerto Ricaness", any type of patriotic acknowledgment. Display Puerto Rican flags, talk about the island's independence, or sing patriotic tunes were prohibited, and that had a significant impact on the development of Puerto Rican culture and more so in Bomba. What Don Jesús remembered was of great importance to be able to understand the depth of risk and courage that it took to play Bomba in those times, to defend it and not be caught by the police and become a political subversive. Bomba was also gagged, and it almost disappeared. Bomba already had a history of being music that incited revolts in plantations in the past. It was a music of resistance among oppressed people, and during the 50s, Puerto Rico was being strangled. Bomba could not be played in the streets; it was banned, and the cops would break up any gatherings of black people drumming, which would only happen in poor neighborhoods.

The political, moral, and cultural value that Bomba had for Don Rafael Cepeda must have been like life itself. To have done the work he did with his wife, kids, and even grandchildren was hard. I imagine that the teenagers in the family probably wanted to do other things and were doing Bomba against their interest, because young people have their particular ways of being and thinking; but it was a way of keeping the family together and building their own legacy which meant security for his family and preserving something important for his people and Puerto Rico.

As time went by, Don Rafael Cepeda noticed that his son Jesús had an inclination for Rumba. Don Jesús Cepeda said: - *"Papi se dió cuenta que a mi me gustaba la Rumba y estaba tirando pa' ese lao' y un día me jaló y me dijo: Mijo, siéntate ahí que tengo que decirte algo. Yo me he jodido para defender esto y la Rumba se defiende sola, cuando la Bomba se defienda sola pues entonces. Papi me hizo jurar en un tambor de Bomba que yo iba a dedicarme a defender mi cultura, el honor y sacrificio que ha hecho esta familia por defender éste género. Ahí yo recapacité, es verdad y metí mano con el compromiso y corazón hasta el sol de hoy."*

Heavy is the head that wears the crown, and for sure, Jesús has been wearing his with style and honor. I find it beautiful that such a powerful moment of bondage, an intimate father-son moment, and also a huge responsibility was given to a young man to protect our roots. That experience was unique. I hope others can find something in this work that can make them understand the profoundness of how little things that might seem insignificant at times and are even unwanted can keep the identity of a nation pumping, the history of people's relevant, relate to other people and be a door that leads them to find themselves while keeping our culture with love and respect. It is important to know the trajectory of what, how, and who has made things happen so younger generations can have access to this art. As we continued conversing about the movement, Don Jesús Cepeda shared some wisdom regarding the importance of being supportive of the cause. He said: - "*Cada cuál tiene que tener su oportunidad para contribuir si lo hace de corazón, y es mejor que haga algo dentro del género, aunque sea mal hecho, porque si está metío adentro, y se deja llevar, se puede arreglar y eso es mejor a no hacer ná.*" I also agree with his statement. We all were beginners at some point, and we all moved forward to pursue a vision of expansion, but the difference was the access we had to our elders and the respect that sometimes seems to diminish between generations. There is a generational gap, but mostly in values that take away from the relationships that are necessary for this socio-cultural practice. I worry for those who do this without any regard for the shoulders of those whom they stand on to represent Puerto Rico without skills, history, or even a personal experience with an elder who can guide them through the process. It is important to bridge generational and cultural gaps to ensure that Bomba survives but mostly its spirit and authenticity.

Don Jesús is a great teacher. He is sociable and shares his family's history and his talent with everyone. His work is ongoing, and although he could afford to be exclusive if he wanted, he has chosen to teach those who approach him. He has been careful not to become this exclusive, unreachable maestro because he knows that time is moving fast and what was important a minute ago can disappear the next, and that being exclusive can cause Bomba teachers, masters, leaders, or whatever you want to title them, to stay behind and forgotten.

He continued telling me about his group *ABC*, and his experience with Salsa music. He recalled Ismael Rivera "Maelo", y Rafael Cortijo's musical fusion with Bomba. He mentioned something very important that impacted younger generations of that time which was the impact that TV had on society and the arts. He loves music and that world of sounds and harmonies. I wanted to ask him how Bomba sounded now versus back in the day, and he put his hand on his chin, his eyebrows furrowed for a moment, and said: -"*La Bomba tiene su lenguaje, su cadencia, tiene su sabor. Cada ritmo tiene su forma y manera de interpretarse y es un trabajo donde el bailador tiene que conocer la música para saber cómo va a aportar. Eso va de la mano. Antes no se tocaba tan rápido y la Bomba no lleva todos esos golpes de rudimentos que le meten ahora, que es una metralleta de golpes. Ahora todo es a las millas y no se aprecia el ritmo, no hay espacio para el bailador lucirse porque todo es acelerao.*"

Bomba is influenced by time, space, lifestyle, trends, and every environmental thing imaginable, including social media. The trend is "Just Do it," but being carefree about doing Bomba, which is still part of our national folklore, can be damaging, and there has to be a limit depending on what we want to achieve with it. If the purpose is to create a national "global" Bomba, then we have achieved it already. If it was to make it accessible, we have done that too. If it was to use it as a creative tool, that has been done, but what should not happen is to be irresponsible and use it to make up a persona and auto proclaim a title when people have not put in the work or have the knowledge to teach this.

Bomba's richness consisted of the variety of regional rhythms and dances that are disappearing. Now Bomba sounds the same, everyone dances the same, and there has been a mixture of regions where now it is very hard to appreciate the differences. Although we mostly see this in the dance, when it comes to the music, the speed has also deformed many Bomba rhythms and styles. The speed sets the tone for what a dancer will do, but besides the movement, the feeling that is meant to be a part of the experience cannot be fully appreciated when everything is so fast, and the main purpose of the dancer is to catch their breath instead of collaborating and creating. The same way that Don Rafael Cepeda made his son swear he would dedicate his life to defending Bomba, those who consider themselves teachers have the same calling and responsibility to teach properly and preserve the sounds, language, and movements that are the foundation of this genre. If things need to speed up, that is fine, but knowing how to slow down and the proper technique is important because when things are always fast, sometimes they cannot be understood or enjoyed. Well, speaking of traditions and feeling a bit of a rush in my heart, I asked him what his thoughts were about women playing Bomba.

During the Bombazo movement and my contributions to that era, I never felt any type of resistance or exclusion by men when I was a dancer, and later the director of the first female Bomba group in Puerto Rico. I must say I never led Nandí, which was the name of the group, with the intention of bashing men or disrespecting them. I learned from men and women and founded, and directed this proposal at a time when I could not afford to exclude men from it. I smiled and dared to ask his opinion on women drumming and being in the forefront of Bomba, to which he smiled, looked at me and Denise, and said: -*"Se rompió la tradición. Antes eso no se veía y no tengo nada en contra y creo que es muy bueno, pero se rompió la tradición. Es un movimiento que ha crecido y ahora el problema es que no dejan a los hombres tocar. Yo no sé si antes las mujeres querían tocar y pensaban que no se les dejaba, pero yo veía a las mujeres bailando y cantando, pero no tocaban. Ahora tocan Bomba, tocan Plena, y lo hacen bien, pero a veces cantan cosas que ofenden y hay que tener cuidado. Yo apoyo todo eso y me gusta ver como la Bomba crece. Esto ha llegado lejos y hay que apoyar todas esas iniciativas y ayudar. Acá en San Francisco, las muchachas siempre buscan aprender y yo con gusto enseño lo que sé y las ayudo para que echen pa'lante y hagan las cosas bien y suenen bien".*

He kept smiling, and his expression was like when you think you have seen it all, there comes that curveball that changes the game. I think he is such a modern man, and I understand his concern about preserving tradition because between evolutions, fusions, and all these new things, if no one has the foundation and explains what the tradition is, then it will be hard to explain where the evolution came from. There has to be a beginning to understand the process, and also the end when each initiative reaches its goal. It was a powerful moment for me to have the blessing of one of many conversations that we have had during our time as an extended family. There is respect, love, and a constant exchange of history that makes our relationship a very meaningful, professional, and loving one.

We had a special time, and spoke about other stuff that I decided not to include here, but I finally asked what he thought was his legacy in Bomba, which he paused for a moment. There was a brief silence that I felt in my heart. I was in front of a living legend, and for a moment, I was not sure if I should have asked that question. I thought about his work, his dedication, and most of all, the confidence and strength he must have to share his family's treasure with so many people. It must be a hard task to share his family's stories and things that made them close, love, fight, laugh, sing, and dance while teaching people from El barrio and all over Puerto Rico, the United

States, and the world how they loved their Patria and their blackness. The conversation did not end there. I talked about something else, but the reply to the question of legacy, I will share later on.

Sometimes, we sit around muses that inspire us to think, observe, and listen. A few months after that conversation, we met in Puerto Rico, and like always, in those brief conversations but filled with so much emotion, he was expressing that as much as he has the patience to support and go along with others in their learning process, he feels upset when people dance without the respect that Bomba deserves. He expressed that many times, he has felt the urge to stand and walk away because it hurts him to see what people do without the thought of not only who they are doing it in front of, but also what Bomba means to him. I felt his pain and frustration and saw his eyes water, and that, to me, is also priceless because I feel honored that he can be honest with me. I share this not to be indiscreet but rather to teach something to those who call themselves teachers. Before teaching a dance step and before teaching a drum slap, please have respect to the elders that are still alive, the memories of those that preserved Bomba, and do not think for a moment that others are not watching what people are doing and will not call you out, on the bs.

I thought about a song for all of us who were, are, and want to be a part of this experience of Bomba. The same way he posts songs that he makes up on the spot, I too came up with this coro en ritmos de sicá que dice asi: *Hubo un ayer, los ayeres de la Bomba, pero el tiempo sigue pasando y seremos parte de eso también.*

Thank you Jesús Manuel Cepeda Brenes. Sin barriles no hay Bomba, sin artesanos no hay Bomba, sin bailadores no hay Bomba, sin tocadores ni cantaores no hay Bomba, sin negros no hay Bomba y sin nuestros mayores no hay recuerdos ni historia tampoco. Este poema es para usted en agradecimiento por esa conversación y el amor grande que le tengo.

Para Don Jesús Cepeda:

Yo soy Bomba
Soy el golpe sentido en el alma
que viaja por una materia contemplada

Manos
Alquimia
Pasado
Presente
Cuerpo que se esparce entre curiosidades ajenas y tierras distantes.

Ancestros, códigos que solo yo entiendo.
Manos que construyen cuentos de madera
Historias que vibran infinitamente
Pinto en sonido el movimiento de musas danzantes
perdidas en trances.

Momento que creo en el universo
Energía
Luz
Secretos en un batey frente a la diosa del mar
con permiso de mi creador.

Yo soy Bomba.
La defino, la transmuto, la revivo con elegancia y cadencia.
Libertad regalada en cada golpe de tambor,
Persigo al cimarrón
marcó su paso para que sienta la tierra
Cierro los ojos para marcarle el camino
al espíritu que busca libertad.
Soy el golpe sentido
Soy Jesús, el misterio de la clave, lleno de Caridad,
Hijo de Rafael
Jurado en el tambor de mi patria
Jesús Manuel.
Yo soy Bomba.

Part 12

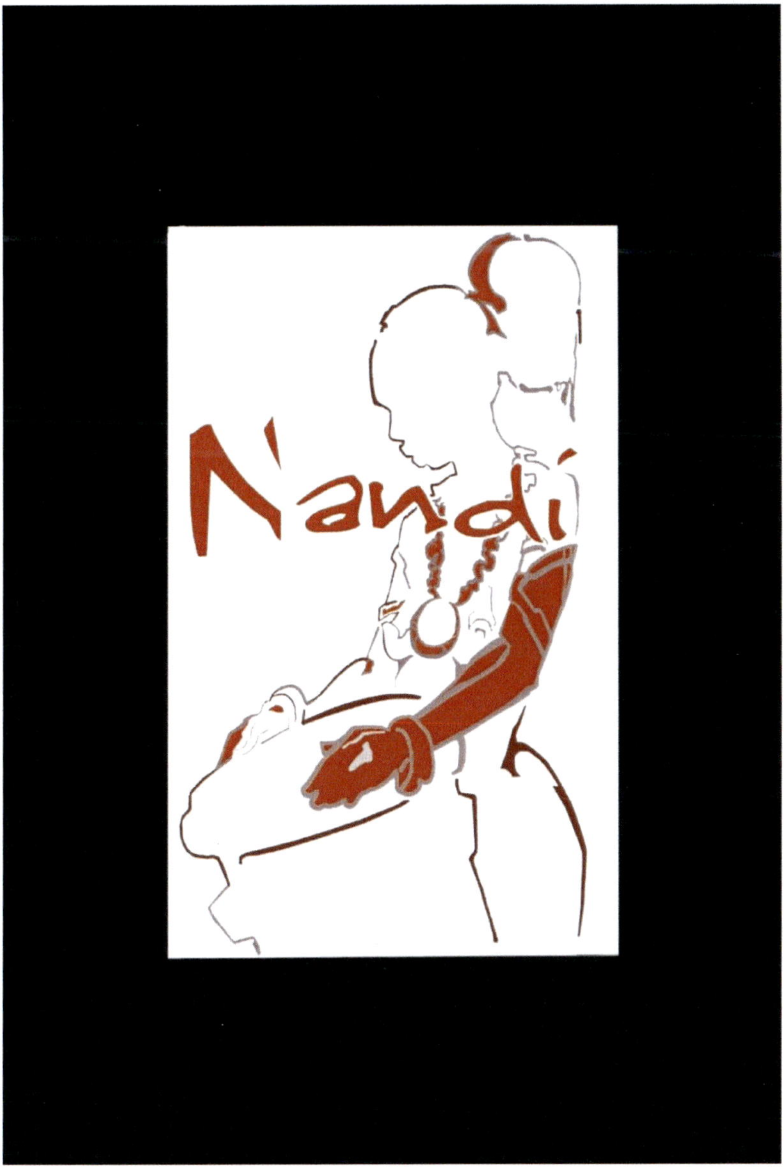

Nandí

Nandí

Breaking traditions

"Camina Nandí, Nandí mamá, tócame la bomba, dime como va". Lírica original Ilia Correa, composición y arreglo para Bomba por Jerry Ferrao.

I grew up resisting being a follower because I was born in a place where I heard constant narratives of leadership since I was a kid. I enjoy working collaboratively, and share what I know and have, but it is not in me to follow others. There is a difference between supporting and following. I will support others as long as I feel I need to, in things meaningful to me, and most of all if it is something that has a greater purpose, and without ill intentions. When the universe changes things for me I don't put up any resistance, mainly because I believe things and people should evolve, and everything has a determined time to be, and for people to do what they were meant to do.

What I follow is the guidance of a higher power that gives me the discernment to know who and what causes I should support, lead, or step back from. I also think that being an only child for the first eight years of my life helped me learn to enjoy my time, and doing what I wanted freely without any control, except for the one my parents had over me. I grew when every social movement was meant to break order and traditions, so maybe, unknowingly, I have been conditioned to create change and with that comes many risks, responsibilities, and lessons to learn. Leaders usually become targets of many negative things because change is not always easy to accept or understand.

Every now and then I reflect on the things I have accomplished thus far to evaluate their status. I take a glimpse to know which ones are still productive and which ones no longer serve a purpose. I think we should do the same with traditions.

The conversation I had with Jesús Cepeda made me reflect about traditions and the roles we all play in improving them or keeping them untouched. Bomba is one of those traditions that besides being art, it is folklore and we should not forget that. Bomba is also a socio-cultural response that forms different types of behaviors, and there is a psychological dynamic happening that is controlled by society and the conditions of the environment. I thought about the work I did with other women that broke a tradition, and that he and many others were not expecting, especially in Puerto Rico.

When learning folkloric art, we repeat, we pay attention to cues, responses, and the rewards involved in preserving these traditions, to mention a few. Our egos are involved in these experiences and they also play a role in the development of these practices that at some point became art, but before that, they were just social and cultural expressions of groups of people that were under-resourced, oppressed, affected by the system, and communities that also have a history of dysfunction and trauma. There is a strong link between our identity and these practices because they represent us. There is a repetition of narratives, songs, dances, proverbs, and most of all beliefs that affect behaviors. There will be a constant practice of behavioral patterns that depending on our maturity, education, and understanding of our roles in society, each individual should evaluate what they do, and how they are doing things, to know what is worth preserving or what needs to be disrupted. We all need to be aware of how folklorist can become accomplices of hiding and preserving social and personal dysfunctions behind Bomba, Plena, and other folk expressions.

Folklorists should think of starting new projects with values that improve the spaces where they choose to share their artistry, improve their professional ethics, but most importantly they should improve to inspire the spectators who look forward to belonging to those artistic communities. Folclór es memoria. Some artists in this field choose to stick to the traditional ways of doing things and representing them which is fine, and others have chosen to do something different, but founded on traditions that serve as a creative platform. I see my work, and especially Nandí, as a memory of a journey that has not yet reached a final destination.

Y Jesús dijo; - "Se rompió la tradición". Mea culpa. I broke it with other women who believed that it was the appropriate time to propose something different. When doing something for the first time it has a different meaning and feeling than for those who continue the work. When materializing an idea, there is a great sense of care, and the process of creating something can be very difficult when there are other people involved. Whenever I think of an idea, I immediately think of three things: How, for whom, and what for? The answers to those questions will determine what I will end up doing, and with this particular project I thought it would be worth it.

Speaking with an elder and listening to his perspective regarding the work that women are doing was important to me. He admired that many women are drumming, and that they have contributed significantly in the proliferation of this genre. He admitted not seeing that before in all his years in Bomba, and overall, a genuine satisfaction with this movement, but also a great concern. His concern had to do with exclusion, bashing and generalizing men's character, and how some songs were offensive and distasteful. This observation made me think of an event I attended in NYC. A member of the Bomba community there shared a similar opinion with me, and also left the venue because he said he could not support how Bomba was used as a detractor by feminists to insult men. I understood and respected their opinions. I also understood the many reasons why that was happening.

In both occasions I could have responded with a feminist rant about women's rights and how they too have been excluded in society. I could have mentioned hundred of songs where women are degraded, and how historically women were not even allowed to play women's roles and men dressed up as women instead. I could have clapped back, as they say, with plenty of facts, but I chose not to, and decided to listen critically to understand where this "evolution" was taking Bomba, women, and relationships between people in different Bomba communities. The impression of the work I did with the women who were the first to go on stage with me for the first time, was not what he described. Looking back at our work, we never held back when it came to expressing what we thought, but I believe there was an understanding of the importance of respect, good taste, and how to use these platforms professionally so that others also respect us, as women and artists. Looking back took me to the beginning of this Bomba's Girls Trip to change.

Once upon a time in New York City, a group of women began drumming Bomba before Nandí. They drummed Bomba and Afro-Dominican music. The group was known back then as Las Yayas, and was directed by Manuela Arciniegas, whom I had met through Alex LaSalle in 1998. After Yaya sang and drummed on different platforms in NYC, Puerto Rico had its first female Bomba ensemble in 2005. We met, prepared for a year, and in 2006, under my direction and the collaboration of an intergenerational collective of talented women, we took a creative chance and became the new image of Bomba. We became Nandí.

In my cultural work I have mostly collaborated with men. Those men that I worked with included me in a mission of making a new Bomba, starting a new movement, and they encouraged and helped me get Nandí started. They helped us by teaching us, lending us drums, writing songs, teaching us about Bomba compositions, talk about their experiences, and sharing their feedback to help us improve.

After we were ready, they helped themselves in many ways, because they would reach out to members of my group to play with them.

The original members were: Amarilys Rios, Melanie Maldonado from Chicago, Priscilla Renta from New Jersey, Layannie Rivera and her grandmother Lydia, Constanza Navas, Maritere Martinez, Beba Febo, Ilia Correa, who sometimes could not join us because she lived in San German at the time, y ésta servidora. Later, others came and went, because for women things are usually more complicated than for men, and I had to work around those complications, as I too had to handle mines. But in retrospect I must express that I will always be grateful for the people who were there when we started what today is a movement that has become a norm.

I started the work with an understanding of what our purpose would be. I had experience in this artform prior to starting this project, I was older than some of them, I always had conversations with my elders, and I had a different perspective about Bomba as an individual. Nandí was a feminist proposal within a Bomba tradition. This meant that control, money, space, power, visibility, and opportunities would have to be shared with women. I did not see this proposal as taking over anything or competing with anyone, because it would have taken too much energy away from me. We created something for ourselves, and added a new chapter to Bomba's story. Now there is a herstory, that in my opinion, does not have to devalue the work of men to validate women's contributions, or ignore other women who have also helped this art to thrive in other ways. This work is supposed to be about a bigger purpose, which is to give our ancestros a voice, to remember them, and that includes our African ancestras, the mothers, the sisters, and all women who left us a legacy.

We were able to accomplish what we did because men helped us and there is no shame in admitting that. Bomba is about teamwork and that was exactly what happened. There was no radical agenda, and I strongly believe that what makes communities and society stronger, productive, and better is the acknowledgment that everyone matters and are necessary in this world. It was a hard task that without their support it would have taken longer or it might have been harder. I believe that the same thing happened in NYC.

Nandí was a means of representation for women who used an important platform, which was the stage, to reaffirm our presence in the arts, in Bomba, and Puerto Rico's cultural events. We were documented in photographs, videos, paintings, and songs that portrayed us as powerful contributors of this art in the new lyrics that women were composing, at least until I led it. Nandí also changed how people in Puerto Rico defined Bomba drums and how they were usually represented. We shifted the traditional idea of representing drums as an object that symbolizes masculine energy to what I might define now as a non-binary instrument.

Hago un paréntesis aquí, because I feel I need to be clear on something just for the sake of clarity on my end. I need to say that when I use the word woman, I am talking about biological women. How biological women identify themselves is not my business, but because I directed this project with other biological women, and we experienced the struggles of doing this while being mothers, working, and dealing with all the hardships we must face to thrive in a society that hardly ever gives women anything, and we must fight for everything, I feel I cannot leave this detail up for interpretation. I strongly believe that what makes Nandí's work important, is precisely because this work is about women, biological women, their contributions, making history in Bomba's evolution, and the changes they made in a social and cultural structure in Puerto Rico that impacted the economy, created jobs, and have done so many other things that have enriched Puerto Rico's culture. Everyone who have added to that story is appreciated, but this is not about gender identity. I believe that is another subject worth discussing, that is equally important, but I will leave that to other people who have more experience in that matter, and are members of the LGBTQIA+ community who have done significant work in Bomba and perhaps can share how Bomba has impacted the ways members express themselves withing these different identities.

La tradición se rompió. Mea culpa. I was part of a Bomba movement that had already broken many traditions and this was another way of adding to that story. The only thing missing in those proposals in Puerto Rico were women in the drumline. We wore the traditional hats, and did what was expected with the exception of leading a group where women were at the forefront in charge of everything, including the drumming. Nandí became an initiative of a modern Bomba that spearheaded a movement that has kept going to this day.

La tradición se rompió. As a dancer, I did both, traditional and contemporary Bomba, and both experiences helped me choose the way that Nandí needed to be represented. She needed to be a part of a Neo Bomba movement. Nandí was modern, fashionable, tasteful, strong, beautiful, and free. Nandí owned that and more. She was not going to use anything to cover the identities of the first women who challenged tradition. I knew that once we did our first performance, we ran the risk of either being loved and accepted, or hated and banned, and I had worked too hard to get to where I was. We put in the work and the rest became herstory.

That journey was life changing. Nandí ended our routines, and also taught us that the further people wanted to go, the more rooted in tradition they needed to be. For me, the process of developing Nandí, meant being closer to my elders, letting them guide me, and work with those who had more experience than I did. I took care of a lot details and registered the group in the Instituto de Cultura puertorriqueña, and in less than a year, we had a name, a certification that acknowledged us as the first female Bomba group in Puerto Rico, we had a repertoire, a theme song written by Ms. Ilia Correa, who later became a member of Bomberas de la Bahia in California. We also had a logo designed by the visual artist Yehimar Ureña, the blessing of my elders, the support of the Bomba community, and the eyes of a lot of women who got inspired by our work.

Nandí was not meant to sound like a men's group nor have a similar energy. I had to share that several times with men who, although had good intentions, did not understand the difference because, in my opinion, there is one. I am not saying that women can't play as intensely or hard as men, or that they cannot do the same things, but there are differences that favored us and I wanted to explore what new things we were capable of doing. I wanted Nandí to sound authentic, and as women we feel things differently than men, and our music needed to reflect that. We began writing our own songs, that some were funny, others were about heartbreaks or looking for love. I believe everything was done keeping in mind that we served a community that also served us. Nandí's process included men that I invited as special guests to play the primo drum in our first performances while we got our primo affairs in order. That move bought us some time for Amarily to prepare for that task. After maybe three performances with that support, she felt comfortable enough to do it herself and instead of guests, we just shared space after our second set so everyone who wanted to play could join, but we made sure we did our work first.

Amarilys became the first primo drummer in Puerto Rico. Besides her perseverance, talent, and enthusiasm, I believe she also became the Bomba drummer that she is, thanks to the many men who coached her and believed in her. Back then there were no women who drummed that could teach her, so men did play an important role in our work

The stage also played a huge role in this story Nandí. If we had just practiced in a park or somewhere without the power of the stage as a platform for representation, the effect would not have been the same. The stage of El Museo de la Raíz Africana was where we made our debut. We decided to dress in white with accent colors. We all looked beautiful, and although we were nervous, we were happy to be able to perform for the first time with no guests. We were in a museum, with our music, for our people in an event that honored women. The place was packed, and I remember looking at the audience and seeing the guys. Mis amigos Bomberos were observing with a smile on their faces and also somewhat judgmental of course. The same guys that helped us get there, rooted for us. Some of them were: Omar Sánchez, Héctor Calderón, Jerry Ferrao, Junito Febres, Angel Reyes, Otoquí Reyes, and Victor Vélez. I also remember Iván Dávila, Papo del Valle, Tata Cepeda, Awilda Sterling, Harry Rexach, Elsa Costoso, and other artists who also attended the event. That experience was possible thanks to the support of Jorge Negrón, who at the time was the museum's coordinator.

It was a special moment for all of us. It was history in the making. We opened our performance with our song, Nandí. As song that Ilia wrote, Jerry fixed, and spoke about Africa, drums, courgae, warriors, Bomba and women. Later that evening, I invited Victor Vélez and Angel Reyes to join us on stage, and Victor sang. Tata and I danced, and Angel played the primo. The event was more than what I had envisioned for our first performance. After that evening, people started talking and spreading the word about what they had seen. They saw the first women's Bomba group. It was a memorable event themed around the abolition of slavery and black women. I will forever be grateful for the opportunity to perform and celebrate freedom and black identity. Nandí, the name that called me, was Shaka Zulu's mother. Her story moved me and resonated with the work we all chose to do. That day I felt as if Nandí herself had blessed us with a dignified way of coming out into Bomba.

In retrospect, I don't even know how I was able to do all the things I did at the time, along with the other women who also had so many responsibilities. Nandí, like in Bomba dance, placed women in the center of a circle that also changed the politics of Bomba. Our bodies on stage doing what we did changed everything. The stage has always been one of my favorite educational places. For this reason, I wanted the stage to be Nandí's space for visibility, and that was what I was aiming for. We accomplished many things that I am proud of and we did those things in a relatively short amount of time. As we celebrated on several occasions the abolition of slavery, I knew that a time would come when I would have to let go of Nandí. I had another calling and I knew that I had to follow it with the same commitment, trust, and love that I had put into Nandí.

Life determines the completion of a cycle and our purpose in different stages of our lives. I had to prepare for a different type of dance, a different drum, a different group of people, stage, and energy that was more ancient than Bomba. Life was preparing me for something new that needed me to take a step back and let Nandí continue walking to where she needed to be. I let go of Nandí before we even stopped performing to accept the new things that came into my life. While others might not have understood, nor did I need to share the details of a personal process, I chose to follow my path and like Julia de Burgos, "Hice mi propia ruta" as I have always done with my life. I left everything to meet with someone new.

In March of 2009, I planned the last gig for Nandí as I prepared to be initiated in La Regla de Osha. I had my Santo crowned, as some people call it. It was not my plan to end the group, but I needed to pause because the universe had a lot of things to say, and I had agreed to listen.

When Shangó entered my life, Nandí left. He and Oshun showed me a new path, a different purpose, and also gave me advices that helped me redirect my life. We met, we danced, and he told me what to expect from that moment on. My orishas informed me about what God had for me. Time confirmed their words, and there has not been a prediction that I have not seen manifested. The advice was on point. Everything was revealed in due time: the good, the future, what others thought they were doing behind my back, and even what might have been considered bad news, became old news before things manifested. What might have been unfortunate became a blessing to me, and I do not regret the choices I made, which also had to do with a future move from Puerto Rico.

Meanwhile, in 2010 Paso Negro became the source through which my blessings manifested. I focused my work as a teaching artist, and as a musical event producer. As an Iyawo I organized one of my first Paso Negro events. I directed and produced *Silhouette*, an homage to Puerto Rican black women and their contributions to contemporary Puerto Rican history. The event took place in La Galería Nacional in Old San Juan. On March 6th, I planned to celebrate my new life and professional identity. It was a multidisciplinary event where I celebrated the achievements of various Afro-Puerto Rican women who had impacted the arts, academia, politics, and Bomba. This time, the music was an all-male ensemble. My son Aris Benítez, Héctor Calderón, Héctor "Tito" Matos y La Máquina Insular, Enoch Carmona, Paoli Mejías, Victor Vélez, Hiram Abrante, and other musicians that together performed Plena, Afro Cuban music, and Bomba. Dicky Colón, a professional Salsa dancer, and close friend, danced with Awilda Sterling, and Enrique Cabrera, a Puerto Rican artisan, exhibited his latest work featuring dolls depicting Bomba dancers.

There was a beautiful exhibition of Norma Salazar's paintings, which was a collection she titled: Orisha. The women who were acknowledged that evening were: Norma Salazar for her work on the book about Catalino "Tite" Curet Alonso's compositions and her visual art, Ms. Nelie Lebrón for proposing and achieving the approval of the first Bomba curriculum in the Conservatory of Music of Puerto Rico, Maricruz Rivera Clemente was the director of COPI which is a cultural and educational center in Piñonez and was running for major at the time, and Dr. Marie Ramos Rosado. She had been approved to teach the first college course on Puerto Rican black women in Puerto Rican literature.

Puerto Rican black history was kept relevant through the efforts of black women, and I had the honor to celebrate that with them, educate others about their work, and do all of that while I was still during my year of religious initiation. In doing these projects I was going back to my roots that were not necessarily in Puerto Rico. It was a different type of understanding of my negritude that I had known since I was a kid. Paso Negro became my new identity, and a means that helped me produce a body of work to this day. I produced other events like *Blackground* in La Respuesta where I was able to bring together a lineup of great artists. That evening William Cepeda, Willie Otero, Paoli Mejías, Richie Flores, Héctor Calderón, Ricky Soler, Enoch Carmona, Otura Mun aka DJ Nature, Victor Emanuelli, Aris Benítez, and other musicians made that evening magical and were called La Fania de la Percusión by a reporter of the newspaper El Nuevo Día. Later, in 2013, I fulfilled something I had in my heart for a long time, and that was to bring to Puerto Rico women from the United States to perform with a collective of women from the island. El Teatro Arriví became the space for that unique Bomba experience where Manuela Arciniegas, Inés Mangual, Cynthia Renta, Denise Solis, Jamie Pérez, Miledys Santiago, Julia Cepeda, Lionel Villahermosa, Maritere Martínez, and I joined the stage and I called the collective Nandí. I chose to call it like that not as a repetition of a concept, not as a goodbye, but as an act of appreciation to what that spirit of courage gave to all of us, including Lionel Villahermosa who was also part of that event. It was an act of gratitude to all the women on stage,to the men who supported all of us in our work, and also as a tradition breakers. All of them been a part of Nandí in different ways.

In the audience, Jesús Cepeda and his son José Cepeda were there with close friends supporting Julia Cepeda. To my surprise it was also the first time she performed Bomba outside of the family and with a group of women. William Cepeda performed with his Jazz ensemble and I was lucky to have him because he was super busy. He was going to be honored in the Heineken Jazz Festival the day after my event. Also from Ponce, El Barrio La Cuarta, Angel Alvarado performed with his group Esencia. Other Puerto Rican women who had contributed to literature and visual art were honored at the event as well. The visual and plastic artist was Annex Burgos, known for her sculptures of the Aguacates in La Placita of Santurce and the Muses in front of El Centro de Bellas Artes joined us, the Afro-Puerto Rican writer Yvonne Denis Rosario was there celebrating the publication of her recent work: Capá Prieto. That evening, we dressed in pink because we were supporting breast cancer awareness month. There was a table with educational pamphlets with information about breast cancer prevention in the lobby, and there was a beautiful exhibit of the visual artist Ms. Yolanda Velazquez.

I could not ask for more; the event was a success, and it was another step toward other new experiences that the universe had for me. We had an after-party that, needless to say, was as crowded as could be in La Hoja. Many great things happened in those few days. I gave closure to many things after that event and began putting my affairs in order because I was making arrangements for a new adventure. In May 2014 I moved to New York City, and from teaching in public schools, I began directing educational programs.

Paso Negro followed me, and I followed the advice of God through my Santos. I had created spaces, and left spaces to arrive at new ones, where dance and music become prayers and religion. Places where tongues are twisted, and flags are worn. Spaces that feel like home, making people feel safe, loved, and whole. I arrived to a place that welcomed me with new faces, new dreams, and a different type of puertorriqueñidad that is also genuine, and purposeful. I went back to my roots, my NYC roots. I went back to an identity that is questioned, challenged, and kept alive on its terms and unapologetically. A raw identity that teaches the truth because we all live in the belly of the beast. I entered a known space where I was born that I visited frequently, and that was mine. New York City called me back to live a new stage of my life, to do and learn new things, and to expand my creativity at my own pace. Life did not want me to settle, and I made my move. Yo no me quité, I decided to continue my work and do Patria for myself and for others. I entered this city like when I do my paseo in a Bomba dance. I took my time, looked around, and waited for the beat that called my spirit. I took the first step to what would be a series of turns. I made new traces on the ground that I walked on once. I live at mi paso, negro, lleno de ancestralidad.

Looking at some things I had put away, I found this message I emailed to the women who performed Bomba in the last Silhouette event I organized in 2013. I called it: Creadora de la patria. I felt the need to share this message with them because we had started a movement that seemed unappreciated, yet it has multiplied and given women, Bomba, and the female energy that walk with us a voice. I dedicate this to the women who are currently doing a great work on keeping our people feeling loved, united, and healthy through music, dance, and most of all presence. The message read as follows:

We have a bond, a responsibility. We have a calling that most likely we didn't choose, but it chose us. La Patria chose us. Not everyone does what we do, has achieved what we have, and knows the sacrifices that we make to keep this going. We stand by that calling, and we stay in the fight even though it's hard. We keep going, facing fears, bullshit, prejudice, and all sorts of things that could easily make us fail and give up. We jump over piedras de tropiezo, unfortunately placed by other women, but yet we continue planting seeds in the hearts and minds of those who need a Patria, a home, a safe space, and support. We are the force, the energy that makes our cultura viva. We are the ones who give birth to those ideas, actions, and people who will identify themselves as puertorriqueños and caribeños. La Patria chose us. Our ancestors knew they could count on us. They knew we could be their voice. We are the reason why our flag is proud. We are the reason why our ancestors celebrate and join us in each drumming, in each song, and dance in our bodies, pushing us in a circle of energies. I am happy and proud of sharing with all of you. I am proud of doing Cultura, nonstop, and with my son beside me, like most of you have done and continue doing. I also appreciate having all of you by my side to create another memory. We have let our ancestors know that the pain they felt and the hardships they went through were not in vain because their spirit and energy live within us. Somos agricultoras de comunidades de gente que son extensiones de nosotras. Sigamos pa' lante con nuestro arte, la fe, y el amor hacia lo que hacemos. Que Nandí siga caminando y junto con ella y la Bomba, todas las mujeres que han tomado un tambor y le ha dado otro golpe, otra voz, y ha creado una nueva historia.

Maferefún Shangó, mis Egun, e Ifá con su sagrado oráculo, donde no existe el secreto, ni la ignoracia.

Ashé.

Part 13

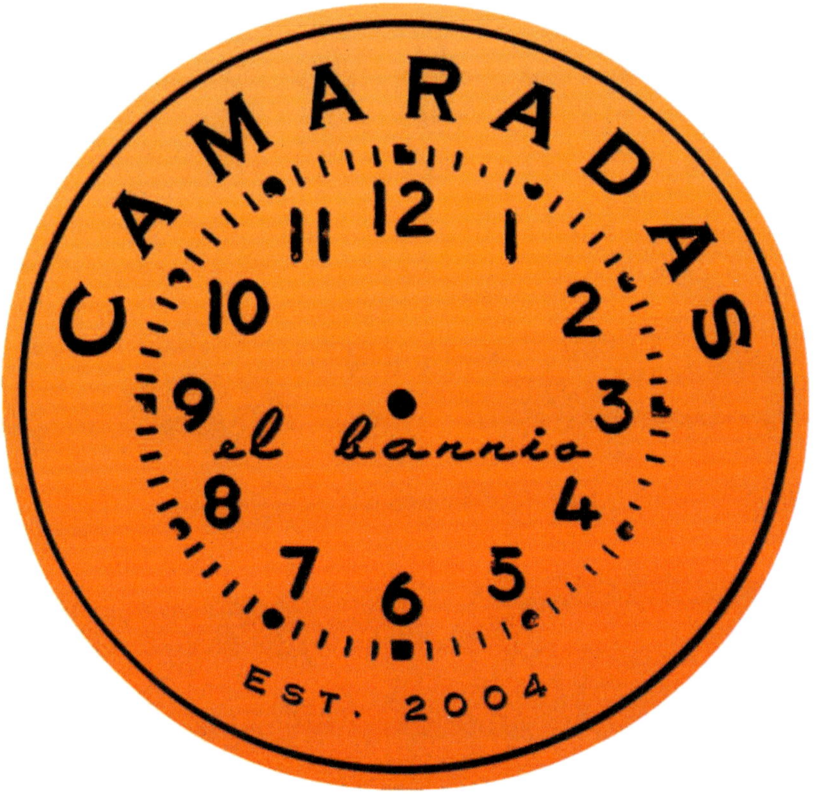

Found in Space

Found in Space

I found a space in New York City. The name of that space was Camaradas, El Barrio, on 2241 1st Avenue, in East Harlem. Mr. Orlando Plaza, the former owner of Camaradas Bar and Restaurant, shared a moment of his time to talk about how that amazing place in El Barrio came to life. Although a lot of people knew him, I am pretty sure not many knew how hard it was for him, as a business owner, to keep a business running and the serious responsibility that it takes to look out for the safety of everyone in that space, and to make people feel happy while trying to make money.

Camaradas was like Cheers, a place where everybody knew your name because they were family. It was a place where people celebrated culture. They celebrated being Puerto Rican, a place where we played Bomba and Plena, Salsa, Hip Hop, House music, and other kinds of music that transformed Camaradas from a bar into a sacred place. Orlando once said sarcastically and laughing: "I'm the only business owner that made a bar into a non-profit." I found it funny but knew what he meant. Business owners have to pay attention to so many details that the least of their interest is to care for the cultural needs of a community or cultural legacies. Those concerns should be addressed by those who do culture, not business owners, unless that is your business. What they need is to make a profit to be able to stay in business, try to get back their investment, and then try to live off their business, but for Orlando, things were different. After fourteen years, he decided to close Camaradas, and after some time, I asked him if it was okay to talk about the experience of creating it, but most of all, I wanted to know the history that led him to open a bar that transformed so many lives. We met in The Market on Essex Street. We had lunch, and we started talking about other things to ease the anxiety. I asked him if he was sure that it was okay to talk about it, to which he replied that it was, but that it was always a little hard to talk about Camaradas, especially when he closed because he had to and not because he wanted to. I had to be mindful and let him know how much people appreciated what he did, all the great things he let people do in his space, how much people loved him, missed him, and what he stood for. I thanked him on behalf of the people who saw him like family and not just like the Camaradas' owner. We spoke in Spanglish, although English is his first language. I began talking about the people who visited Camaradas, and although they had conversations with him, most of us did not know about his experience and motivations aside from Camaradas. I was interested in knowing who he was besides the man who ran the show in East Harlem. I asked him to tell me about himself, specifically the things that had to do with his identity. What experiences influenced his national identity and professional goals?

He did not hesitate and replied: -*"As far back as I can remember, I knew I was Puerto Rican. My parents were proud and had contradictory narratives of Puerto Rico. For my mother, Puerto Rico reminded her of pain and hunger; for my father, it was joy and fun. She was from a rural town, and my father grew up in an urban city. I was born in this city and grew up with these competing narratives, and I cannot explain how, but I knew we were colonized as a child and that white people were the other. My interest in the restaurant business was because of my father. He used to like to take us out to eat, and he would take us to Restaurante Andalucía in Chelsie, and the place was run by a Spaniard guy named Joe. He was a host. I remember he made me feel at home, and he used to call me "El gallego". My grandfather also influenced my life in some way. He had a lechonera in Mayaguez. I've always liked the idea of running a restaurant. I like that business because of how the people there made me feel. Later in my adulthood, I worked as a bouncer in the Dew Drop Inn on Perry Street and Greenwich Avenue. It was a Southern-style bar. I fell in love again with the business. The staff, the bar, and how everyone moved were like a show. They were in the theater business and were actors, and their personalities influenced the business. It made me think, you know what, Orlando, you can do this! The Bar business is a theater. That was what it taught me. Another place that had an impact on me was Agueybana Book Store, run by Scery Colón. It was a space of gathering. A place where like-minded individuals got together to discuss politics. It was a place to meet other people and focus their energy. I met the poet Mariposa, Flaco Navaja, and Tato Torres. It was a bookstore that only sold books by Puerto Rican writers and had a performance space. Sery became an intergenerational bridge. I met Tato Laviera, Miguel Argarin, y a*

Perry Thomas. Another place that influenced my vision was the Nuyorican Poets Café. At a time of gentrification, los Migueles, Miguel Piñero, and Miguel Argarin claimed their space. It was a time to ask where were the Puerto Ricans. They emphasized the importance of space in a city where space is contested. They made the word Nuyorican a self-identity marker of empowerment by publishing a book. They claimed their identity as Nuyoricans and defined it. Another experience was when I worked in an original Irish pub. It was a blessing, and I learned that the Pub for the Irish is as important as a church. They call it the local, and that is the nearest Pub. When I was a student of History, I learned that there were spaces in the pubs called smigs. They were spaces within the bar where people could gather, like semi-private rooms to the bar where the clergy would go there and drink with privacy. I was fascinated with the whole history of Irish Pubs! It was a place to drink, to commensurate, and to conspire. Pubs became supporters of political movements for uprisings. They became political sites". - As I listened, I was also observing how his anxiety went away and how he enjoyed remembering those moments. He seemed as if he missed his father, how much he liked Joe, and how this robust man welcomed him into his place when he was a kid.

He understood the importance of connections and how the bartenders turned each evening into a type of Teatro de lo absurdo, as he put it, engaging the public/clients in a different world that helped them forget about what was going on outside. The mix of recreation and information, culture and relationships, and the awareness of himself in a space with others that needed one, informed his thought of seeing himself plantando bandera somewhere, somehow, someday.

-Orlando, qué hacías antes de tener tu propio negocio, what were you up to before thinking of Camaradas? *-"I was studying to do my Ph.D. in History in African Diaspora while working as a director in Clemente Soto Velez Center after Ed Vega's resignation. We decided to create a cafe with an aesthetic of the working class and the history of New York City. We chose to use metal, brick, wood, and industrial material."*

-What motivated you to have your own business? -*"It was a joint decision between me and Raúl Rivera, a friend of mine. We both supported each other in the idea. We spent years thinking about it and discussing it, and we took that chance. We had no experience in business management. We had no money either. It was during the Clinton administration's UMEZ program, Upper Manhattan Empowerment Zone, and loans were given to people who were interested in opening up a business, and I applied for one. We were approved and then unapproved. Then, another friend, Jay Zhao, came into the partnership. He told me to forget about the government loan, and we did things in another way. He knew about contracting and looked for investors. I thought about many things in the process, like: Do I manifest this desire for my career as a professor or risk it all and become a Restaurant/bar owner? I thought I could do both, but that's not how it worked out. I took a leap of faith and threw myself completely into Project Camaradas. I have no regrets."*

-What did you sacrifice to achieve your goal? -*"My Academic career and maybe my stability."*

-How did the name of the business come about? -*"Camaradas is a combination of Carmen and María. The name of my mom and Raul's, but when we decided on that name, I also understood the political connotation and how it related to the socialist movement. At the time, Raúl was reading a book about time and life, and that was the inspiration for the logo. Rafa Merino did the graphics, which, by the way, it's not a clock. It's a gage from a Soviet fighter jet Mig47. There were subliminal messages of revolution. The logo meant we made the time. Another place that influenced our idea for Camaradas was a restaurant on the outskirts of Ponce called La Querencia. I loved that place. It was eclectic and run by a Spaniard who was fucking awesome! He had a little stage. He was a beautiful nut!"* - He said as he laughed, then continued describing the place. -*"He served Sangría, and one time that I was there, I asked him about the stage. The man told me, eso es para cuando vienen los bohemios. He had an open-stage policy, and that was something that I wanted for Camaradas. I didn't want any formalities; I just wanted people to take the stage and do whatever, but it didn't happen that way. One of the things that reminded me of La Querencia was the old mic, and I got one for our stage. In retrospect, I used everything that inspired me and corresponded with the essence of what I wanted for Camaradas."* - He looked relaxed. I believe he enjoyed sharing that anecdote and recreating those feelings. He confirmed, once again, the importance of space for everyone, and if we cannot find it, we must create it.

What was your business proposal for the Barrio? -*"Crear un espacio where people can meet, connect, and claim as their own. We wanted to combine Pub and culture because we're always in someone else's space, listening to other people's music. I thought it would be a good idea to be in a space where people can have a drink and listen to their music. A place where we didn't have to apologize for who we were, and there were no places like that around at the time. To make those connections to your culture, you had to go to Wille Steakhouse, El Corso, and Broadway 96, but those were clubs. I wanted to do something accessible, a Bar like other cultural groups had, but for our people. Another thing that I wanted to do was to focus on doing business with independent beer makers to sell craft beers. I wanted to sell boutique beers, which at first was challenging because the people who went to Camaradas didn't know anything about it. I never wanted to sell those commercial beers, but my customers didn't know how to drink, so I started teaching them about these other beers and made suggestions so they would try something new. Most of my clients were teachers, maintenance workers from NYCHA, you know, working-class people who needed a space to go to after work to unwind. I remember we had a Happy Hour that, money-wise, was miserable, but with patience, it worked out, and I had ten draft beers at the time, and I would give them samples. I love sharing and turning people on to new things. With time, they became beer snobs!"* - He laughed and made a face like he couldn't believe how his clientele had changed. -*" In a year, they knew about flavor profiles and became beer snobs, unbelievable! All of a sudden, they were picky y se tornaron sofisticados!"*.

I enjoyed learning about how he noticed these changes and how he kept them as something dear to him. I told him that even though he shared something I thought of talking about later on, I wanted to know about the dream of Camaradas.

Orlando, háblame de tu sueño. Cuándo creaste a Camaradas, and when did that dream come true? - *"It was during the Summer of 2004. That opening day was a shitshow, yeah. I was good friends with Olga Méndez, she was a real bad bitch, and I loved her, and she earned my respect 100%. She ran East Harlem and part of the South Bronx. Una puertorriqueña imponente, con carácter y estaba en la política. Olga Méndez was a pioneer. She was the first Puerto Rican woman elected as a member of the New York State Senator. Olga was a chain smoker and drank whisky, an original OG that I adored, and there aren't many women out there with the control, passion, and respect that people had for her. I opened Camaradas during an election year, and of course, we had an opening party. I remember that on that day, the band that played was Kalunga, an Afro-Dominican group. The place was packed, and de momento llegaron un grupo como de twenty-five or thirty people. They were led by Olga's nephew. They were part of the Positive Workforce Construction site that hired BIPOC. So, these guys marched in front of Camaradas to disrupt the opening because Olga thought that I had invited her opponent to the opening! That's how serious she was about her shit!* - He started laughing about it and continued with the anecdote. -*" They stood there for a while, and I went to her nephew, and he delivered Olga's message. She thought her opponent was coming to my opening. I told him Yo' you better leave cause this isn't gonna end well. This is not the place for that. This business is a neutral political ground, and I didn't invite anyone here, so stop this bull shit because I have people too. Camaradas wasn't a place for politicians to use as a platform for their gig. I knew a lot of people who were into politics on different levels, but I never identified my business with them. Everyone was welcome in Camaradas as a client, but I wasn't identifying with any political party or agenda. The space wasn't for that!"*

How do you insert the arts as an initiative for your business, and if you can remember, who were those first artists who approached you to use the space for the arts? - *"Claro que sí! I remember Rigo Peralta and Gia did their visual art events there, I also remember Viajero, and for music entertainment, Kalunga used to perform, and then came Yerba Buena. I hope I'm not missing anyone. I knew Tato Torres from Agueybaná BookStore and the Viva Puerto Rico Libre days. He was playing Bomba at Edwin's. He used to pass by the place before*

Camaradas was even finished. We had conversations about the possibilities of him playing, and I told him he would have a place there whenever he wanted. I had a small stage in a corner, which later changed. That was what La Querencia inspired. I didn't think that little stage, which I thought would be an open space for bohemios, would become a spot for the arts."

-How did those art proposals help your business? -*'' Music saved our lives. I don't think we could've made it without it. We opened a business in one of the most economically depressed places in Manhattan. I opened Camaradas, but the community dictated the need for the arts in the space. I was just open to it. The community defined how they needed to use the space, which helped the business, and I hope I also helped them. Live music became intractable. We had groups from different cultural backgrounds, sounds, and genres. There was no way to control it because the artists took control of that part of the business. Music became a signature of Camaradas, especially Bomba. Bomba found a home in Camaradas since the year we opened. I believe those groups that performed in Camaradas were able to get exposure, followers, and do what they wanted to do in the arts, and the community met them and the work they did."*

I have fun memories of Camaradas, and it was a space that felt like home to me. It was a space that I knew I was going to see my friends and Bomba was there for me. When I moved to NYC permanently in 2014, I found a safe place to go to whenever I missed Puerto Rico. I knew I was going to find my home and medicine there. I knew there was my other Patria in a small space that also reminded me of the bars in Old San Juan. I had to ask if, during all those years in El Barrio, he noticed any changes, especially when East Harlem, like many other spaces in the city, was being gentrified. He looked at me and replied -"*El Barrio? Not much going on, only one bar in the corner. The hood, East Harlem, has something that makes it almost ingentrifiable, and that is the geographical fact that East Harlem has the highest concentration of NYCHA buildings of any community in the five boroughs, creating pockets of permanent poverty, and generational poverty. Socioeconomically, the community can't go anywhere. The neighborhood didn't change. Camaradas transformed the energy between 115th Street and 116th and made everyone step up to keep up.*

What other initiative came from your business? -"*Camaradas was very photogenic. People went there to film, book signings, poetry, burlesque. I think I did pretty much everything except comedy because the room wasn't good for that. People identified with the live music and also the days we featured DJs like DJ Bembona, DP One, and many others that attracted a different crowd.*"

What observations can you share regarding how the cultural impact reshaped the identity of your business, and as a Nuyorican, how did you feel about it? -"*I knew, and they knew I was proud of who I am and the work that I was doing. I didn't have to hang a flag or do a mural with palm trees and a coquí. Those were not our markers as Nuyoricans. Our Puerto Ricanness is expressed in a different way. What happened there with Bomba and all the other things that happened cannot be written in a business plan. I love my culture with a passion, and I know why I love it. I don't love a commercial or generic version of my Puerto Ricanness. Bomba contributed to my vision and provided financial support. I was thrilled to give space to something that had to do with our Africanness and that it became a thing that people wanted to be there to see Yerba Buena play Bomba and be a part of that experience dancing, singing, just being there. If I had pursued my studies, I would've been writing about it, but instead, I was living it. I was living the difference between the theory and the praxis. I was doing it. I was creating a space for Afro-Diasporic expressions, no matter where it came from. I was learning and growing with others, and Camaradas, to me, became more than a bar. I believe that if anyone found a place to identify with in Camaradas, then they found their Puerto Ricanness.* –

I agreed with him. A lot of people who went there and saw Bomba for the first time fell in love with it. It was not only Bomba. It was a mixture of a lot of elements. The aesthetic of the space, which he envisioned it in that particular way with a reason. It represented the working class. The corrugated metal that many compared with the tin roofs of the houses in Puerto Rico, and was meant to represent the fences on empty lots, the hardwood floors, brick walls, even the type of light bulbs, everything in the space created the right vibe and inspiration that in the words of Mr. Plaza, -"*It allowed art to become and people to interpret it. I think that the best way to describe that experience is a poem written by Mariposa, our anthem, Diasporican.*"

What precedent did you establish in El Barrio that became a part of the community? -"*Well, one of the things we did was create Puerto Rican Pub food. I wanted to make sure the food was good. It was important to me. I think that our menu raised the bar in that community. Food has to do with identity, and I refused to sell anything frozen, which was economically brutal. I think we proved you can open a business in that area and be successful, but there has to be sincerity in your intent and the way you interact with the community. We didn't dumb down the product. We didn't sell out. We sold good food and good beer, and the entertainment was authentic and badass. It was good as long as it could be. I know people respected me, and Camaradas also made me have some kind of personality there. With time, we grew with it, and people in the community liked me. I think they used me/Camaradas as a model to demand a certain quality from other businesses in the area. The corner was a problem I had to handle. I had to manage challenging behaviors with el Tigeraje. The leaders of the community would come to me because they could, because of the relationship I created with them. They told me that Camaradas had set a standard that had to be followed if anyone wanted to open a bar. We went beyond being a bar. I believe Camaradas left a legacy, an imprint that has become a palimpsest. That imprint might probably fade, but it's still memorable. Everything that happened there was organic, and people felt ownership of the space, which was one of the things I wanted to do with the business.*"-

What were the challenges that you faced in trying to keep your business? -"*New York State doesn't make it easy, the tax structure for micro-businesses isn't favorable. Utilities are expensive, there's always a challenge. The Department of Health chips away at the profit margins. In 2008, Camaradas got audited twice, which never happens with small businesses. I think it had to do with the identity of the place. I felt targeted. NYC is hostile to micro-businesses. One time I spoke to my accountant about it and he said - "Orlando, they, the city, don't want businesses like these anymore. They want the CVS, Dunkin*

Donuts, Walgreens, you know, those types of businesses." Orlando continued explaining that the challenges many of the businesses have to deal with are because the city is changing*."*

– En algún momento sentiste deseos de mudarte del Barrio? -*"Yo quería expandir el negocio. Era una meta que tenía. From 2008 until around 2010, I was exploring Brooklyn. I had my eye on Bushwick and I knew it was the right time and the right space for another Camaradas. I knew what was going to happen there because it coincided with the exodus of Puerto Ricans from the island. A community was growing there that could've been receptive to the concept of Camaradas. We tried, but it didn't happen, and honestly, I took it hard not to be able to do that. I knew that was a good opportunity for the business and also that things were changing for Camaradas in El Barrio. The reason why I was considering having another spot was that gentrification hurt men business-wise. I began losing a lot of people who were part of the core group. A lot of artists were forced to leave the neighborhood, and Brooklyn was becoming that new place to be and where the arts were flourishing. It was hard. Anecdóticamente, there was a strange thing that used to happen in Camaradas. Every four years, the customer base changes in Camaradas. It felt like graduating classes, synonymous with school. Every four years, the group changed. After its ten-plus year mark, I had lost the core group from when Camaradas started."*

- When did you know you had to close the business, and what confirmed it? -*"Well, you know, when things started getting harder, and I didn't see a solution anymore or a way out of the financial situation. The crowd also changed and in the last four years, it didn't transform in the way I needed. If anything, it got worse and I was getting customers that were elements I didn't like. People come in, users have their habits, and use the bathrooms to do their thing. I didn't like how Camaradas was changing and what it was becoming."*

Camaradas left an imprint. Camaradas became an entity, and I guess it chose when it was supposed to retire. I asked him if he felt supported by the community during those times, to which he replied with a question

-" *Community is several things. I know the leaders in the community loved me and I built good relationships with them. I knew the community board and they liked what Camaradas was doing, but in the end, it was a lonely venture. I get people coming to me almost daily, asking to do this again, but they don't know it almost killed me."*

People do not see the struggles and how a person's health can be affected terribly by all the stress and disappointments when managing a business in this city. I admire that the same way he decided to open and do things on his terms, he closed Camaradas in the same way. I wanted to change the vibe and asked if he remembered any famous people who might have visited Camaradas. -"*Yeah! We had a lot of people stop by like Eddie Palmieri, who loved our alcapurrias. Also Malcolm X's daughter, Malikah, the poet Willie Perdomo, Dylcia Pagán, ex-political prisoner, and the actor Matt Dylon. He used to love Camaradas. Also, ex Young Lords would come to visit, Bernie Williams, the baseball player, Arturo Schomburg's grandson, the delegation from Venezuela, the actor Esai Morales, Tracy Morgan, and the artists that performed and created such a wonderful experience there with their artistry."*

Cómo se puede ayudar a conservar estos espacios tan necesarios? -*"By patronizing it, paying the cover, consuming. It's a profit venture; there is no other way. Perhaps getting sponsorships, but it doesn't make a significant difference."*

Well, I want you to tell me the three most important things you learned as an entrepreneur. - *"Wow, I never really took the time to think about that."* - He took a moment to reflect, and after a few minutes, which I did my best not to rush the moment, he answered: -*"Well, nothing is as easy as it seems. I learned to take responsibility for being a leader. There's no substitute for sincerity and integrity. They should be the core values of anything you do. And difficult things are worth doing."*

- Tell me three ways in which Camaradas formed your identity as a Puerto Rican -"*Camaradas gave me the opportunity to create a space, un espacio para expresar al máximo mi puertorriqueñidad como yo la concibo. Fue un espacio diaspórico antes de que se pusiera de moda la palabra y fue mi tésis doctoral en praxis"*- What are three memories that you cherish from Camaradas? -'' *Besides opening the place, I remember when I held the meeting to brainstorm on how we would participate in the Puerto Rican Day Parade. We came up with the idea of the Ilustres, which was awesome. Another great memory is when we planned Camaradas's 10th anniversary. We formed Camaradas Salsa Orchestra led by Desmar Guevara. That evening, DJ DP One was also part of the event, and at some point, he battled with the timbalero. Another thing I remember dearly is the Halloween party we used to do for the neighborhood kids."*

- Orlando, dime una sola palabra, just one word that you believe would describe the essence of Camaradas?

- *"Revolutionary".*

Part 14

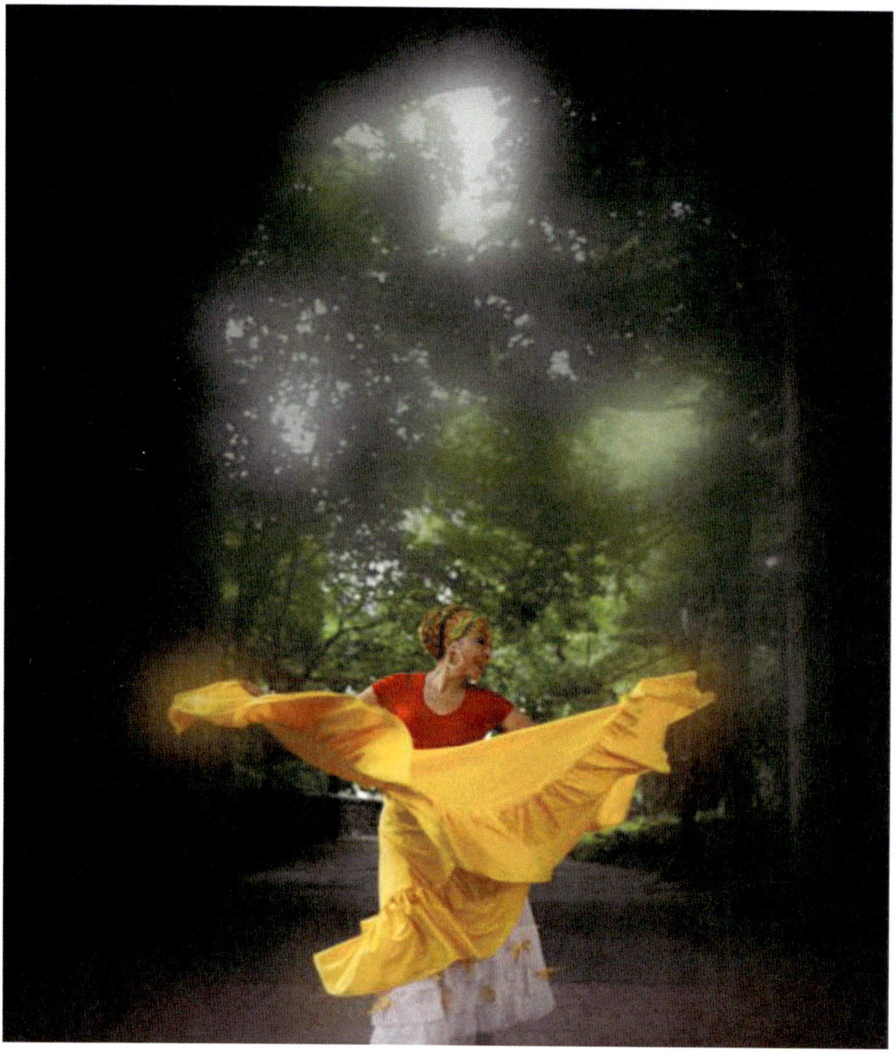

The Dance of circles

No importa la lejanía, donde suene un tambor de Bomba, allí llegaré para llenarme de vida y rendirle mis respetos a los ancestros que nos visitan atraves de la vibración de barriles que cuentan historias que reaparecen en cada antilla, en cada solar, en cada esquina de barrios negros. Historia sepias, criollas, mulatas, y del que deja el pellejo casi blanco en una esquina y se para frente al tambor porque todos tenemos un ancestro que nos jala por el pelo y nos lleva frente al pasado para que lo miremos de frente. Ese que nos centra y nos mira para que bailemos, cantemos, sintamos en el cuerpo una identidad ambigua a causa de la colonización y nos re encontremos. Allí, en el lugar donde gritan: Habla! En medio de ruidos, silencio, y movimiento, reflexionamos. Allí, en medio de golpes que resuenan para despertarnos y levantar a los que habitan bajo la tierra y bajo el mar, y en coros y repiques suena el eco de lamentos de la España que el Moro invadió. África en España, ambas en el Caribe y negras todas y todos y todes respondemos a la Bomba que nos llama para entenderla, vivirla y contarla. La contamos en baile y coros unísonos de un pueblo que aún resiste. Yo soy Bomba porque la vivo. Yo soy Bomba porque la comparto. Yo soy Bomba y Bomba es Patria, y la Patria se hace.

Bomba gives the dancer the opportunity to be both a dancer and a drummer. The movements that a dancer does are interpreted musically by a drummer whose experience, skills, and knowledge of a traditional musical language produce a sound that represents the movement, the step. This interaction happens simultaneously. The sound is not produced after the step has been done. The drummer needs to be familiarized with the dance to be able to predict, based on body posture and preparation. The drummer also pays attention to the step or series of steps that the dancer will make to respond at the same time and in sync with the dancer. Bomba is a dance of observation and listening. Bomba dance is an outward expression of an inward understanding of music, movement, awareness of the body, time, space, energy, and the capacity to transform any of those concepts within a timeframe. There is no way of dancing Bomba without a plural concept of self, but it is necessary to find oneself and understand one's body and the response to the beat in order to do all the other things that Bomba dance requires.

Bomba dance gives me the satisfaction of feeling and hearing my dance. It is a custom-made series of movements created by what inspires a dancer when they find themselves in the center of a Bomba circle. Those personal steps are inherited and interpreted by the dancer in collaboration with the drummer who plays the Primo or Subidor Bomba drum. This particular drum is supposed to be played by someone who masters the skills, knows Bomba music, and understands the dance. Traditional Bomba steps, those movements that belonged to our ancestors and were passed to us by our elders, are repeated over and over again. When the movements are interpreted musically, it creates a particular musical language that, although they sound unique or "Puerto Rican", they are also similar to other Afro-Caribbean and Afro-Latino cultural musical sounds, which at the core of it; what we hear are the sounds of Africa. The corporeal movements executed in Bomba dance become an improvised musical composition, a musical articulation that can either enrich or damage the musical base or basic rhythm that creates the musical foundation of Bomba music and for Bomba dance. There is always a possibility for change in this art because Bomba also represents the socio-cultural evolution of a people in motion in every sense of the word.

Bomba is a dance that has to do with personal energy, musical understanding, body language, and a reciprocal inspiration between drummer and dancer. Like my mother says: "Al que Dios se lo dió, que San Pedro se lo bendiga."

It is not Bomba's purpose for people to lose their identity, but rather to define it, help the person explore it, understand it, and empower it. Bomba dance is an encounter with awareness. The body takes in different musical stimuli that provoke a corporeal response where the person who is dancing, the drummer who is playing for that dancer, and the people around the dancer become one and create a collective experience.

Bomba dance is not disconnected from the emotional and psychological state of the dancer. This dance can be used to check our state of mind, emotions, and stored traumas and notice how our bodies might have probably changed in the ways we move due to physical injuries or inactivity that have modified our postures and ability to move. All of these things are part of the discoveries that can happen when learning to dance Bomba if the teacher knows how to observe the needs that the students arrive with. As a Bomba dance teacher, I do not teach this art as a Zumba dance, copy what I do method, or teach choreographies so people think they know how to dance right away. That is not how I learned, and I think that people miss out on so much when they leave with an easy pass to Bomba dance ciphers and don't get to experience their truth in movement, and all the other meaningful things that Bomba dance can give.

Bomba is the dance of listening. I believe that it is important to prepare the body and mind for listening before we dance Bomba. This process might be difficult because of the habit of instant gratification, where students want to dance like a professional after one or two classes. Listening is key in this dance, not only to learn about Bomba history and to learn the music, but also to be able to listen to oneself in the middle of that musical and dancing collaboration. It is a collective work that, to be in sync with what others are doing, people need to listen to one another. The usual focus will always be on the drums, but people need to learn to listen to the other minor percussive instruments that play an important role in Bomba music, and also serve as guides for the dancer in case the drumming is not on point. Experienced dancers will know how to read the room and hear the room, and with their dance, they will also know how to start to communicate to create what seems to be a conversation but really ends up being a collaborative monologue.

Bomba dance breaks the predictive dance pattern that is seen at the beginning of what we call the stroll or Paseo. If we interpret this in other ways, Bomba dance also breaks the predictive behavior that colonized people display and is reflected in their improvisation. What breaks the pattern is the complexity of the dynamic that happens in the musical interpretation of an individual dance. In Bomba dance, there is a constant exchange of interpretations. These interpretations are related to rhythms, movement, history, society, norms and behaviors. Other things are also a part of these cultural exchanges like ethics, community, identity, how people learned this art, and most importantly, the struggles of the coexistence of the past and the present while trying to ensure that Bomba exists in the future. Bomba is structured but also breaks away from it through improvisation.

Bomba dance consists of two basic parts. The first part of the dance is a stroll that creates a pattern. Besides the stroll or Paseo, what comes next is a series of movements that, although improvised, are a collection of traditional movements that are called Piquetes. These movements are repeated by everyone, they have meaning, and they also represent regions, genders, and tell a story, like any folkloric dance. These steps are also supposed to be genuine expressions of an individual and not a clone of another dancer.

For anyone who has never seen a Bomba dance, people usually stand in a circular formation, and in this setting, no one is excluded. Everyone plays a part of what is going to happen. Everyone is necessary, whether they are observing, dancing, singing, or deciding to play an instrument. If the person decides to dance, they move from the spot where they stand and take a stroll towards the center of the circle or dancing area using a basic step that has been traditionally assigned to a particular Bomba rhythm. This stroll or Paseo has many different meanings to me because besides being a literal stroll through space, it is also a stroll through different dimensions where the past informs the present and is expressed through dance. The dancer strolls inside a circle where old sounds and chants, like muses, prepare the dancer to feel in tune with what is going on around the dancer but, most importantly, what is happening within. The paseo is done with the intention of listening and preparing the body. The dancer gets in tune with an inner beat that guides and warns.

I have learned where in my body that beat lives and where the energy that makes me move is stored, but to be able to do that, I had to learn to listen and dance with myself first. In the Paseo, the dancer should be aware of how they feel. They should know how to create a mood, or if there is one already, the dancer must know how to either fight it and change it or flow with it, depending on the dancer's need and also the collective need. During the Paseo, the body, as a recipient of all its life's experiences, finds a way to channel that energy in the middle of a circle where they are creating a different space for themselves. The time when the dancer does a stroll should be respected, and the energy and mood that the dancer is working on should not be interrupted because it is during that time that the dancer sets the tone for what will happen next as a result of that readiness. Little things that usually interrupt that flow are abrupt changes of songs, drum breaks when they aren't needed, switching drums that might cause the energy to drop, and people talking loudly around the dancer. No matter how this stroll is done, which can be as simple or as dramatic as the dancer wants to make it, it is a moment of representation of the individual, their identity, a nation, and the idiosyncrasies of a people that have been labeled as marginalized and all the stereotypes, misinformation, judgments, and history attached to black people and what they do. During this part of the dance is where the dancer organizes in their body, mind, and spirit a concept of time, space, energy, shape, and overall elements of dance while in movement. It is during the Paseo that the community that is engaged has to support the person who is in the center of that circle.

Buleador drums, which are the ones that drummers use to produce a basic, constant rhythm, are the ones that create a musical foundation from capo to coda and back to the beginning; Buleadores will not change only if there are musical breaks, which are usually done for performances. The sounds of the Buleadores, when played well, they can be so rich and perfect that sometimes a Primo drum is not even needed. They are responsible for providing the dancer with that blank musical canvas for the dancer to start decorating with moving pinceladas. This is why I do my paseo with respect because it is more than just my presence and my dance. It is a moment for me to create a connection and communication with something other than me that lives within me, and connect with everyone in the space. The paseo is done constantly during the whole execution of the dance because although it is more noticeable at the beginning of the Bomba dance, the Paseo is what stitches everything together. The constant basic step throughout the beginning, during the improvisation, and at the end of the dancer's piece is what creates a sense of continuity in that foundation, and what creates a connection that, although silent because the Primo drummer does not play any beat for basic steps, it helps make sense of the musical composition by allowing the music and drummer to "breathe". The Paseo becomes a way for problem-solving because it gives a dancer time to think about what to do in their improvisation and prepare the body for it.

During the Paseo, I am getting ready, and I also look for momentum. A momentum that is felt, not forced and provokes to respond with a natural, spontaneous, but controlled movement that will also determine the amount of energy, attention, and tension that I need to produce it. That first golpe, that first movement that demands a simultaneous musical response, is called Piquete, and with that first

Piquete, we begin to create our personal, improvised dance. Yo empiezo con uno. I start with one movement that demands one beat because in my articulation, in my dance and message, "I", "Yo" am the one who will start communicating. That first movement later becomes a "we" after everything blends in. Unlike other dances, no specific story is told that others can read into it, as in Indian dances. Bomba is the dance of feelings. These feelings will change as the dancer begins to improvise, and with the help of the other Bomba elements that may vary even during the execution of the dance.

In Bomba dance improvisations, we create contrasts; some have meaning, and others do not. It is what we call in Danza, "Motivos or coremas" which are sequences or sections, segments of movements used during the improvisation. Bomba dance improvisation has to do with a combination of the basic steps, the traditional and cultural knowledge of movement that is stored in the body through repetition, and the ability to let creativity flow. Some of the concepts that are related to this process are what we call "motivos''. These motives are stored in the memory, which is created during the learning process in praxis. We use these movements in a predetermined way to create spontaneous choreographies and musical compositions. Because this practice is repeated from generation to generation, it can look similar, but every dancer will make these old steps look and feel brand new depending on how they perform them. These patterns and combinations acquire a collective meaning and define the space and people that make them. This is why la Bomba de Loiza is different from the Bomba dance of the South, and dancers and musicians from each region should know how to interpret them because they have gained an understanding of the importance of the particularities of the different styles that represent places, people, and their history. They should know how their particular Bomba style sounds like.

Style is what differentiates dancers and reflects how the dancer organizes their dance according to their level of mastery. Su ``forma", and the musical language that the dancer creates, is a product of a musical understanding, and body movements that go with those sounds. If the dancer does not know the Bomba language of the region, then it will be difficult to create a style where the body can respond to the foundation that the drummers have built for the dancer. The dancer is responsible for improvising in tune with the drummers, according to the Bomba region, and also being able to show their personal and artistic style in their dance. When a dancer is not familiar with the musical language that corresponds to the Bomba style of a region, it will cause a musical dislocation or deformation. To avoid a musical disaster that will affect the energy and collective dynamic, the Primo drummer will "fix" it by not responding musically exactly how the movement requires. The lack of the musical Bomba language and awareness of how the dancer sounds will not help them improve their dance, but it is something that should be fixed in class, and not in social activities. Again, I need to ask, who is teaching, and how are they teaching?

To "fix" a Piquete for a dancer in a dance class is to leave the student in the dark, and that is why listening is key. Not every dancer has the competencies to communicate with their dance or has basic knowledge of the clave. Bomba teachers should ensure that their students acquire a clear musical understanding, and keep in mind that they are also doing a different type of drumming with their body movements in their dance during the improvisation.

Bomba dance can be very complex, and to what has been mentioned, I have to add the aesthetics. The aesthetics in Bomba dance are details that are also connected to style. In Bomba, this is created with how the skirt is manipulated, posture, how arms are extended, and the way the dancer creates figures that also balance the body because of the closeness of the patterns of the footwork. Gestures, facial expressions, the positioning of the body before doing a Piquete, and the corporeal, and musical conversation that the dancer creates require an aesthetic, especially for performances. After all, Bomba is art and as that, it should be beautiful. That is one of the things that makes a great teacher. How they prepare their students to be great dancers, musicians, creators, and do all of that looking beautiful.

When dancing for an elder, there are expectations that have to do with definition, strength, intensity, a variation of speeds, swag, what we call "guapería" but with elegance, coolness, and most of all, control. The dancer needs to know how to listen and also have a cool head to not let the music take them away. They expect the dancer to create dimensions, use levels, and know how to move in the space and make space if needed. Back then, whoever danced Bomba had a complete mastery of all the things mentioned above. Dancers like José Cámara, Perucho Cepeda, Roberto Cepeda, Tata Cepeda, Alba Cepeda, Raquel Ayala from Loiza, Petra Cepeda, Angel Luis Reyes, Otoquí Reyes, José "Nuno" Calderon, Junito Febres, Maribella Burgos from Loiza, dancing the style of Loiza, Maritere Martinez also a Loiza style dancer, and Vilma Sastre, are a few of those dancers that I believe meet all those requirements in their particular Bomba regional styles. They did not skip a beat or miss a space in the music. They enriched it and increased the energy and tension for the spectators. They were known for their style and Piquetes. These movements are done with an amount of energy, precision, direction, and intention, where the dancer needs to find the proper posture and maintain balance. When dancing with a skirt, that posture will also require accommodating the skirt as a prop to follow the body and become an extension of it. The initial posture of the body also changes from the moment the dancer is doing their stroll to the moment they start improvising. This happens because the types of movements that will be done during the improvisation will require the dancer to shift their weight to perform the steps, and manage the struggle to balance levels, and use of force to keep the energy required to execute elevated or low movements. Also, they need to control the transitions while keeping the same energy from the beginning until the end of the dance in a stylish way. We see dancers do a lot of flexions, the use of the ball of the feet instead of pointing with toes, leg and arm extensions, symmetrical and asymmetrical movements, the rotation of the body, among other natural movements, and most of all, groundedness which is key in this form of dance. There is a constant bouncing that maintains the beat and anchors the dancer. Dancers look for a pivotal moment to begin discovering how they sound and continue a personal dance interpretation. Everything needs to be done looking effortlessly.

Improvisation is the source where we find or create new material, but in Bomba dance, it has to do with new interpretations of traditional steps that maintain the meaning and value of the dance as a folkloric one, and not something experimental although we can explore new forms of old steps. It is also when people can see the personality of the dancer, and how the environment can impact the dance. When we improvise, we explore, we try to push things to the edge, we let our minds go, and we discover, at times, a different story to tell, but weirdly enough, everything is controlled. The dancer can experience sensations and develop images that demand a whole different set of skills to be able to be still while in movement and attentive to the present moment while in the dancer's head, they might be somewhere else. Teaching someone to improvise requires patience and close observation of the student's body language, body shape, strength, and many other things to help the student use everything they have to their advantage. Improvisation is a moment of truth and being okay when feeling vulnerable. When I dance Bomba, I evolve in a space of respect and for fun. Dancing Bomba is a humbling experience that has taught me to work with energy and transform the vibrations that surround me, change myself, and make Patria wherever I go. Danzo en círculos, y en medio de ellos me encuentro y me pierdo.

Part 15

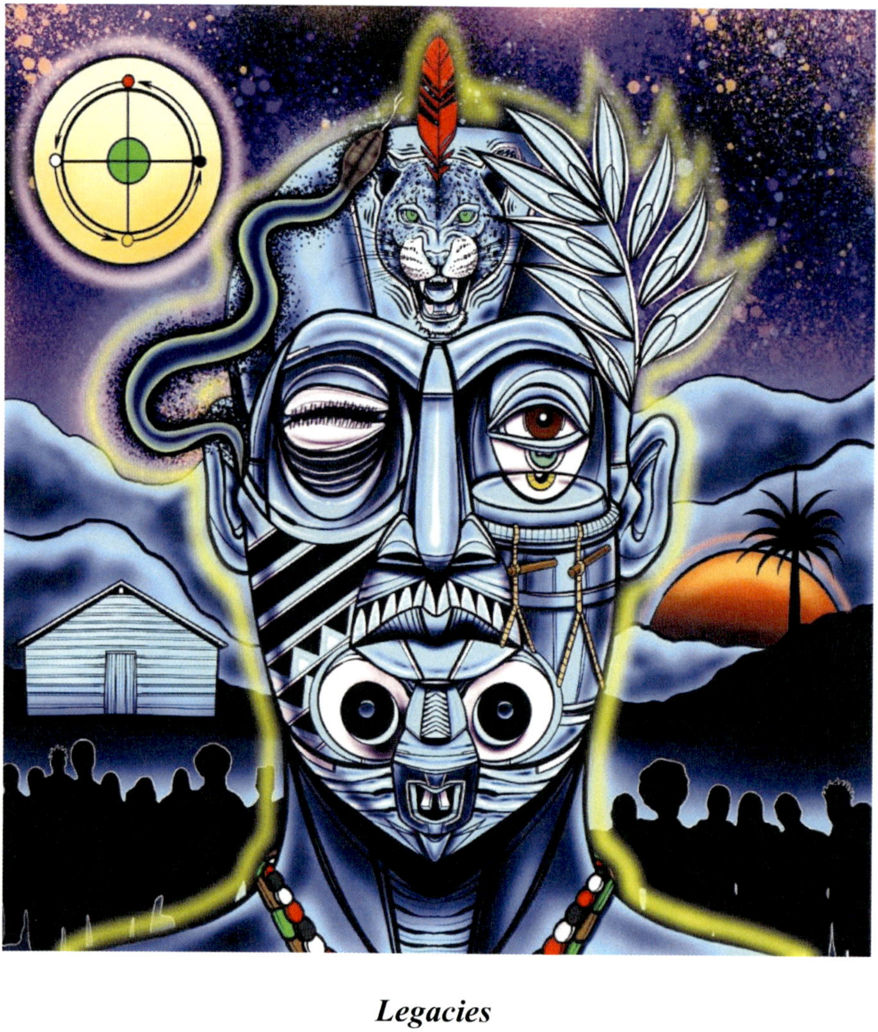

Legacies

The Muse of Legacies

The muse of legacies makes us reflect about our temporary state and our desire to be eternal, remembered, and present. The muse of legacies reminds us to re-evaluate how much we are willing to hold on to the past. The gift of legacy puts a big responsibility on people's shoulders because once a person becomes the voice of remembrance through legacies, part of the life and time of that person is dedicated to making sure that the legacy does not die. There is an exchange and a sacrifice in the act of keeping legacies alive.

I interviewed Alex LaSalle, and I am very grateful that we had the opportunity to have the conversation that we had. I learned about his life with Bomba, his fears, and his fight with death. He shared his vulnerability with me, which made me respect his work even more. I am forever grateful for his sincerity and openness because that is a rare quality nowadays. Alexander LaSalle, is a man who has dedicated many years of his life to doing Bomba in NYC, and has done a tremendous work with his group Alma Moyo. He has also collaborated with many other groups in the diaspora, representing the diaspora in Puerto Rico. He shared how the muses of Bomba and of legacies have also shaped his life and most importantly, have saved it.

Elders like Felix Alduen, Papo Alers, Roberto and Tito Cepeda, and Juan Gutierrez, Chema, among so many other NYC-based folk artists, shared their legacy with him and mentored him. He mentioned others that guided him spiritually, and gifted him with a knowledge that created new roles in his spiritual life. Those roles have to do with leadership, representing others, and dealing with time. He learned how in Bomba, and in his spiritual path, the past, the future, and the present, are connected. In his practice he has found the strength to face and conquer life's struggles, and practice how to Bámbula. I learned the meaning of the word with him, just like many others that use it without giving him the credit.

Alex has allowed these muses to guide him. I guess that is what we all do; we embark on a mission of remembrance that starts with elders, music and dance, with codes and history that eventually everything transcends into a spiritual realm, and nothing is isolated. Recusitamos is a word that has become a muse for him and his family. It is a word that he sings, but in this particular song, he is chanting a truth. *Recusitan* is the name of the latest musical production, and one of his songs. Part of the chorus says: - "*Recusitan entre nosotros los cimarrones de lo tiempos de atrás"*. But in reality, it is us that revive each day, until we pass, and the past lives with us. We need to find that marron spirit that resides within to fight what oppresses us spiritually, and the powers that be. We revive in our spiritual being with the inspirations that unknowingly guide us to the medicine we need, and prepare us to provide what others are seeking in us. We build communities with the gifts that we are given, and create families with whom we all find our divine purpose, and for me Alma Moyo and Alex has been that special spiritual and cultural brother whom I have a tremendous amount of love and respect for. I am a member of the group, his house, and must say that I am proud to belong to the first group that has explicitly defined through songs and drums, the spirituality of Bomba, and what this art wants from us.

Moyo, which means Alma, is a Bomba group that has closed the gap between both realms, the spiritual and the physical. The work of Alma Moyo gave the legacy of traditional music, songs, and dance a new form where the spiritual aspect of Bomba is no longer denied. It is sung, danced, drummed, and prayed. There is no way to deny our ancestor's spiritual legacy any longer because in doing so, we are dishonoring them. There is a new mission, a new proposal that goes beyond entertainment. There are many pieces missing in Bomba's history, and we need to look in other places to find them., but in this search we find that all of the ancient practices that for many are just forms of entertainment, are really medicinal practices. Bomba is for everyone, but that part of it is only for a few. This is something that the universe chooses and not something people can buy, steal, or even understand so easily

Alex had to wait ten years between one musical production, and the recent one to allow life to teach him a few important lessons to testify about the power of an almighty force that, the same way it helped our enslaved ancestors to survive, has also helped him and keeps him standing. It took the fear of losing his life to know that the only way you die is by living, and while you live, you need to do and be who you are meant to be and do until your time is over on this plane.

Nuestro propósito es Sikama Moyo, which means to liberate ourselves and find the freedom we want, which is not in this world, or the experience in the physical body. Some legacies are accepted with the purpose of evolving and were chosen by our higher self, then we forget, and it takes some time to remember what we chose. Art and different practices like Bomba, help people remember, and they guide us back to the right path for us to move up, and not in circles where we repeat ourselves, it takes us up, like a light directed to the sky where we can evolve.

Alex shared memories of his beginnings and how important it was being in the community. A special space for him was El Rincón Criollo aka La Casita de Chema. He shared and learn with elders who had been doing Bomba and Plena in NYC way before he started. He remembered that due to the lack of Bomba drums, they improvised barriles with congas that were cut in ways to produce a similar sound to a Bomba drum. He talked about the color of his skin and how he understood that he knew he had certain privileges, and he knew that Bomba is música de negros puertorriqueños, which he defines as such and always reminds people. He shared a painful memory from his childhood; like most kids have that are raised in this city. He remembered how his mother had to endure the embarrassing experiences that most Puerto Rican women had to deal when people questioned them about their children because of the color of their skin. She was often asked if she was his mother because of his white skin and light eyes. His mother is darker, and people could not understand that, and thought she was his nannie.

Alex remembered belonging to a community of young, passionate people who just wanted to do Bomba without an ulterior motive. Like most groups, Alma Moyo also had members who came and went, but those who stayed have seen how the work has evolved.

We live life within a concept of time, and as long as we think we have time, we tend to procrastinate. The younger we are, the less we think about it and feel eternity in our spirits. The only people who do not have the privilege of wasting time are the ones who know that, for some significant reason, their hours are limited.

When I asked Alex what inspired him to write these songs, his voice cracked, and he said that he decided to work on this musical production because he thought he was going to die. I felt that pain and moment of sadness in my heart, because I know him and his family, and knew how hard that was on all of them. The work in which I had the honor of collaborating gained a different meaning to me. While I looked at him explaining how he felt fear of not being there for his kids, his wife, and his family, I realized the amount of faith, willpower and how his warrior spirit had to rise to overcome the doubts and somehow find a way to continue fighting. He found that strength in focusing on doing the project he intended, manage his health issues, and decide to be present, and live while God and the universe decided whatever needed to happen next. The universe, God, and all the spiritual forces that sustain his spirit have held him and given him health, and it was during the production of this art that he found a way to center himself, to move back to his spot in the Bomba community in New York City, and Puerto Rico, and find ways to heal as he shares his medicine and testimony with others.

I feel nothing but joy for him, his family, and for the opportunity of doing what I have done so far with Alma Moyo. I feel honored to have shared with people who have gifted me with their time, which is the most valuable thing someone can give. I believe Alex's work is not done. Time will tell if the work that we all have put into different communities, artwork, and spaces and shared with individuals will become something worth remembering. He wants people to remember he did his work with respect and love for his Patria and for Bomba.

Creo que sin egocentrismos, ni ínfulas de grandeza, todos queremos ver en esta vida el fruto de los esfuerzos hechos y compartidos. As he expressed that truth, which I align myself with, and agree, I thought about Jesús Cepeda, and something I asked him in my conversation with him in San Francisco.

I will end this work with the answer that he gave me when I asked him what was his legacy to Bomba, which he replied:

-*"No te puedo contestar esa pregunta porque aún estoy aquí trabajando, y estaré hasta que Dios quiera. Cada persona con la que yo he compartido y he sembrado esa semilla de cultura, podrán decir qué les he dejado, pero siento que me falta mucho por hacer".*

And that is how that conversation about Bomba with Jesus ended, and that is how I feel about my cultural work, and how Alex feels about his. I hope God gives me health and ways to keep doing what makes me feel happy. I love to educate, create, and move. I encourage others to pursue their dreams and enjoy the journey of becoming the best version of themselves. I hope they do things with so much passion that they inspire other people, and change someone's life by just being genuine, and true to what they believe in. So far, I have done everything I have set my mind to do, including this written work, which, although it is not perfect, is a perfect way for me to thank my people, Bomba, and the community of dreamers who have given me so much.

Yo no sé qué pasará en el futuro, but there is one thing that I know, and that is that as long as muses continue visiting me and inspiring me, I will continue to give them a voice, and just like my elders, I hope to have the blessing of seeing the seeds that I have planted turn into an árbol que dé sombra para el que la necesite. As I leave this work and other legacies, and gifts to my sun Aris, and his sun Akim, to bámbula me, his grandmother, mines, and all the elders that have also blessed him with their wisdom, love, time, and most of all the gift of drumming, I will wait, live, move, write, and tell the stories that keep my family united, strong, and spiritually connected to a higher power and the muses that are here to inspire us to keep working on the most important legacy of all.. Continuity.

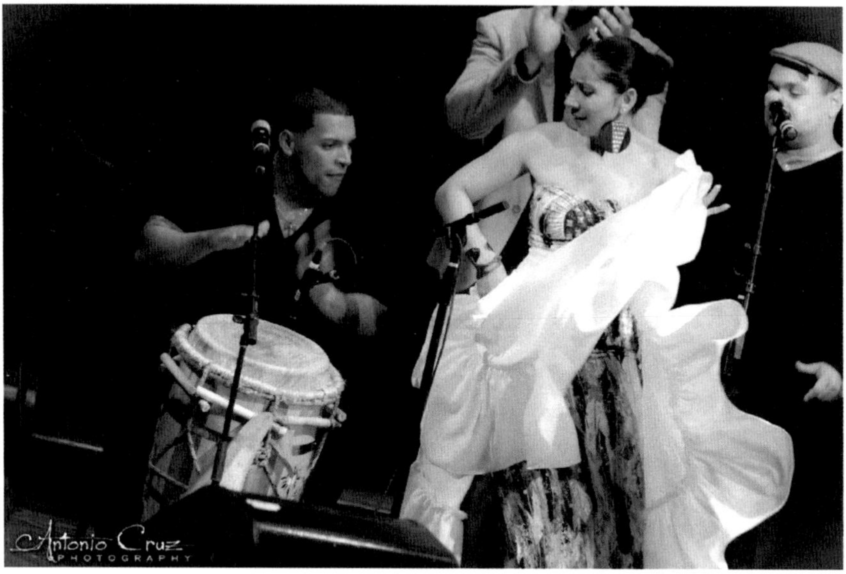

Aris Y Yo